The Therapist's Workbook

SECOND EDITION

SECOND EDITION

The Therapist's Workbook

SELF-ASSESSMENT, SELF-CARE, AND SELF-IMPROVEMENT EXERCISES FOR MENTAL HEALTH PROFESSIONALS

Jeffrey A. Kottler

WILEY

John Wiley & Sons, Inc.

Printed in the United States of America

V10005650_103018

CONTENTS

CONTENTS

INTRODUCTION

It has long been my fervent belief that one of the most remarkable privileges of being a therapist is that we have so many opportunities to grow and learn as a result of our therapeutic work. When I first conceived the idea for this workbook, it was to create a structure for myself to help make sense of everything I was processing as a result of my interactions with clients (and colleagues). Throughout most of my career I have searched for as many ways as are available to apply to myself what I learn with and from my clients. This means being continuously reflective, not only about the clinical work itself, but also how it impacts and influences me personally. There isn't a week that goes by that I don't learn something significant about myself; often this is the result of being challenged by clients, students, and supervisees who ask me, in so many ways, whether I truly practice what I preach in my own life.

I developed many of the exercises in this workbook as a way to help me to assess and monitor the changes I have experienced throughout my life, not only as a professional, but as a person who tries very hard to live what I teach to others. Perhaps like you, I have read numerous books about therapy but find that many of the ideas and lessons don't "stick" for very long. Thus, my intention was to create a reading experience that was far more interactive and engaging, one that requires you to personalize the content and respond so that, at the end, you have a written record of your own development as a professional.

Why Read This Book?

You are reading this book for a good reason. It may have been given to you or assigned to you, or it may have caught your attention because it promises to help you look critically and honestly at your chosen path as a therapist, as well as the implications of this choice. Furthermore, this is not exactly a book that you will *read* as much as one you will *participate* in, through your own active contributions. In that sense, then, *you* are the author of this book because it requires you to write your own narrative, tracking your personal aspirations and professional conduct. I am merely your guide through this process.

During the journey that follows I encourage you to identify and examine what you enjoy most and least about your work, and then set goals and structure plans accordingly to make what you do more professionally effective and personally fulfilling. Even if you are mostly content with your work, this process will help you become more aware of what you do that is most helpful to others and most satisfying to you.

There are several reasons that a workbook for therapists might appeal to you: First, you might be new to the field and interested in learning more about the inner world of helping others, especially about the realities of therapeutic practice. Or you might be a veteran concerned with the stress you face on a daily basis, and are seeking to build more pleasure into your work. I must say that after 35 years of practice, often I find it becomes harder (not easier!) to remain energized and focused on what I do. I become tired doing or saying the same things over and over. I sometimes feel bored just listening to myself, sick of my same old stories. Whereas once upon a time every new client was an exciting adventure and every new clinical problem was an interesting challenge to negotiate, it now seems I am reliving the same sessions over and over again. Obviously, this is a clear sign that I have work to do—and that is what led me to revisit many of the questions I pose and exercises I present in this workbook.

One difficulty in structuring an experiential journey for therapists is that practitioners work in such varied settings—elementary and secondary schools, community agencies, orphanages, charitable organizations, substance abuse centers, hospitals, clinics, mental health centers, crisis centers, universities, government or military agencies, corporations, private practices. (That, by the way, is a list of all the places that I've worked!) Each setting has its unique challenges. For example, those in private practice may have yearned for a sense of autonomy and independence but now feel isolated and torn between their roles as professionals and entrepreneurs, especially during tough economic times. Those frontline social service professionals may enjoy the companionship of colleagues but also have to deal with the most serious, intractable, crisis-oriented cases, often working in less-than-ideal conditions, and with limited resources.

No longer is the typical client in therapy a neurotic, upper-middle-class, white individual who is struggling with issues of angst and midlife transition. More than ever before, we are working with a culturally and economically diverse population, which presents an assortment of difficult problems, from substance abuse and domestic violence to posttraumatic stress and dissociative disorders. In addition, even though the presenting problems are becoming more serious, we have less and less time to help our clients. Brief therapy is the order of the day. Paperwork and bureaucracies require us to justify what we do and then defend our decisions.

In spite of the differences in our disciplines, theoretical allegiances, work settings, and clientele, there are several fairly universal features that are part of almost every therapist's experience. Regardless of your level of experience and professional setting, this workbook is intended to help you:

- Reveal the major sources of stress and conflict in your therapeutic work.
- Renew your motivation, energy, and creativity as a clinician.
- Work through countertransference and intense personal reactions that have resulted from your practice.
- Heal personal wounds that continue to haunt you and interfere with your professional effectiveness.
- Improve your clinical skills, especially as they relate to untangling difficult cases.
- Increase your impact and influence as a therapist.
- Transfer knowledge and skills from the professional domain to enrich personal effectiveness.
- Integrate the personal and professional dimensions of your life in such a way that you feel more fulfilled and satisfied with work and primary relationships.

These goals are certainly ambitious—not unlike those you might offer to your clients, regardless of their particular presenting complaints. Nevertheless, in spite of their broad scope, it is possible to make significant progress toward reaching these goals, to take better care of yourself as a person and as a professional.

The Itinerary

This is a journey we have undertaken since our first training experiences. Initially, many of us felt tremendous idealism and altruism, that as a result of our devotion to healing we would somehow make the world a better place. A bit later we discovered, or at least acknowledged, that we also had some very personal urges that drove us toward helping others—motives not so much related to saving the world as to saving ourselves. Our fears of failure, of inadequacy, of mediocrity, of darkness, of being lost or alone, may have pushed us toward a calling that permits us to feel in control and in charge, at least some of the time. Whereas practicing our profession does fulfill many of the needs and sparks the interests we were looking for initially, over time our enthusiasm wanes. It is only through continual supervision, training, and perhaps therapy or personal growth experiences that we can keep the momentum going. It is in such a spirit that this book is offered. Although it can't substitute for real-life personal growth experiences, it can supplement them. In many ways, there are even some advantages to undertaking this journey in a more private context.

As I mentioned, this is an *interactive* book, one that requires your participation in the process. As you might hear yourself say to your own clients, lasting growth and enduring change take place when participants:

- Reflect on what is being said.
- Personalize the material in such a way that it becomes individually relevant.
- Adapt ideas and concepts to their particular life circumstances.
- Challenge ideas so that they become consistent with personal needs and values.
- Defuse defensiveness so as to remain open to new ideas.
- Integrate new concepts into existing schemata.
- Experiment with material.
- Apply what has been learned in various situations.
- Invite significant others to accompany them on the journey.

This process is, of course, familiar to most practitioners. Before desirable changes can be implemented, and endure, it is first necessary to gain a handle on the nature of the difficulties. Part I of this book presents the sequential steps of an assessment process that will help you to identify specific sources of joy and hardship in your personal and professional life. Part II helps you to resolve identified struggles and problems by addressing targeted areas and suggesting ways to generate more fun and satisfaction in therapeutic work.

How to Use This Book

Perhaps similar to your experience, I have long been frustrated by the challenge of helping people to take what they are learning and make it part of their lives. So often students or clients become inspired by an idea they are reading about or hearing in a lecture or session. They dutifully take notes. They study the concepts, get excited about the possibilities. They then resolve to make some changes in their lives.

Typically, this commitment lasts about as long as it takes to explain what they are doing to their friends or family members, who may be threatened by what is presented. Perhaps you can recall one of your own experiences of returning from an exciting workshop and then trying to explain to others what happened, only to be greeted by yawns or looks of puzzlement. We have learned that most of the time people would prefer that we stay just as we are, and not make waves that would cause inconvenience in their lives.

I would like to suggest a strategy with respect to this experiential workbook. Although you may start out reading the various sections and then thinking about and writing out your responses, ultimately you will want to take this material home, so to speak. In the same way that you try to work systemically to involve a client's family and friends in the support system for planned changes, you can do the same with respect to your own family, friends, and colleagues: involve them in the process.

Along this journey we will take together, I invite you to visit some places that will seem familiar, as well as others that may look like foreign territory. As on any transformative travel experience, at times you may feel lost, frustrated, confused, or impatient. My job, as your hired guide, is to help you through this process in such a way that you remain safe yet stimulated, entertained, and, most of all, *changed* as a result of your efforts.

This all takes time, of course. I realize that time is one thing you don't have in abundance. The last thing in the world you need is to feel like a student with a bunch of assignments to do (although at least they won't be graded).

Nevertheless, as you know and say almost every day, constructive, transformative change requires work, *hard* work, and commitment. So the question remains: How much of yourself, and your *self*, are you willing to invest in this process? How much time are you willing to spend looking at your work, at what you do and how you do it?

Some Specific Strategies

Depending on your own best learning style and preferences, as well as what you need right now in your life, here are several ways you might use this book:

- Take a chapter each week and go through the activities and exercises in it, slowly and reflectively. Treat them as rewards that you've earned, rather than as assignments to complete. Each of the questions you are asked to consider is intended to help you write your own narrative about who you are as a therapist, what you do best, and what you might do more of to make your job and life more satisfying.

- As in therapy in general, it is often the unscheduled, serendipitous moments sparked by sessions that have the most impact. Even in the face of the most elaborate planning, logical sequencing, and thoughtfully drawn itinerary, any transformative journey comes with unforeseen twists and turns and unintended consequences. To take advantage of this process, remain open to what you feel, think, and experience between scheduled writing sessions. It isn't the exercises themselves that matter so much as what they stimulate inside you, sometimes when you least expect it.

- For those of you who are inclined toward more structure (or who have decided you need more of it in your life), make a commitment to supplement this workbook with a journal, in which you pay attention to what you learn in your work every day: For one day a week, after each session with a client, write a brief note about something you learned about yourself and about the way therapy works. Pay particular attention to at least one thing you said or did in each session that you especially liked, as well as one thing you would rather not do again in that precise way. At the end of each week, in addition to completing a chapter's worth of assignments, write down what you learned from your clients about what's important in life and what is most crucial in promoting changes.

Although I have been struggling with many of the issues presented in this workbook, most likely the same will not be true for you. Some of the chapters will appeal to you more than others, and these are the ones to which you would devote more time. I would recommend, however, that you at least review the material in each chapter. As you well know from your own work, people are often quite unaware of the issues they most need to work on—until they find themselves haunted by themes that won't go away.

New to the Second Edition

The Therapist's Workbook was first published in 1999 and has been a favorite of both practitioners and students alike because of the opportunities it provides to explore deeply some of the most pressing, interesting, and disturbing issues that crop up as part of our work and lives as therapists. Although there is considerable value for experienced and even master therapists to review the challenging issues they face each week, newcomers to the field will feel especially supported and encouraged as they review some of the most difficult problems they face. As such, this book has been frequently offered as a "gift" to practitioners; but it is also used as a textbook in a variety of classes in psychology, social work, counseling, family therapy, human services, and related fields.

This second edition retains much of the flavor of its predecessor; at the same time, it has been considerably updated and expanded to cover a variety of new issues. Whereas the previous workbook focused principally on the hardships, challenges, and difficulties of doing therapeutic work, this new edition offers more balance. In addition to the chapters on dealing with stress, making sense of therapeutic work, addressing countertransference, managing conflicts, acknowledging failures, and countering burnout, there are new chapters on appreciating the privileges and joys of what we do, as well as finding deeper meaning in the work and lifestyle.

New sections have been added that help you to: (1) explore the ways your clients can become your greatest teachers; (2) incorporate travel and adventure in your personal life to better inform your clinical practice; (3) increase creativity and novelty in sessions; (4) achieve greater consistency between what you advocate for others and how you practice these skills and beliefs in your own life; (5) broaden what it means to be of service to others by addressing issues of social justice; (6) make doing therapy more fun and interesting; and (7) build a better support system to make changes last—not only in the work you do with clients but in your own life.

Audience

This book can be used as a textbook for classes in social work, counseling, family therapy, psychology, human services, and other related fields. I use neutral language throughout so that content is not identified too strongly as representing one particular discipline, approach, or theoretical orientation. Instructors have used the previous edition for their practica, internships, and field work classes, their theory classes, and introductory coursework, depending on how the journey is framed in the context of student growth and development. The book will appeal to any instructor who would like students to reflect on issues in the field and engage in active learning strategies. It thus lends itself as a supplementary text in almost *any* class in which the goal is self-reflection.

A note to students: Although many of the questions and exercises ask readers to talk about their experiences with various "clients," if you have not yet begun to do therapy, you may instead substitute any helping experiences in which you've been of service to others. Alternatively, since a major thrust of this workbook is to foster greater creativity, I encourage you to use your imagination to construct what might take place for you in the future. Generate responses that project you into the future, when you have logged years of experience.

Traditionally, this book has also had appeal to practitioners in the field who wish to engage in periodic self-analysis and exploration. The issues raised and the exercises presented appeal to experienced practitioners, as well as to beginners. It is the kind of book that school districts, universities, counseling centers, and mental health organizations purchase for all their employees to help them reenergize themselves and engage in a form of self-supervision. Even after so many decades of practice, I periodically review many of the exercises in this workbook to sustain or to inspire my own personal and professional development.

One More Thing You Can Do

I'm as skeptical as almost anyone else about the value and safety of using "self-help" books without supervision and guidance along the way. Perhaps more than most consumers, therapists understand the dangers and limitations of launching a transformative journey without studying good maps of the area, proceeding carefully, and even hiring an experienced guide.

Although some clinicians may prefer a solo adventure in which they complete the therapeutic tasks in solitary reflection, others may wish to integrate what they are doing within the context of their supervision sessions, staff meetings, or other scheduled interactions with colleagues. It may even be desirable to undertake this process as part of peer supervision or an ongoing support group so that opportunities can be created for talking about what is stirred up, as well as for making public commitments for the future.

As should now be clear, this is an interactive book, not one you merely read. To promote significant and enduring growth along your own journey as a healer and helper of others, you will need to talk about these ideas with colleagues, peers, and loved ones. Most importantly, you will need to *act* on what you learn.

Jeffrey Kottler
Huntington Beach, California

The Therapist's Workbook

SECOND EDITION

PART I

Confronting the Issues

CHAPTER 1

On Being a Therapist— and the Consequences of This Choice

Being a therapist has its consequences, for better and worse. On the one hand, you enjoy benefits that accrue to a professional who has devoted considerable time and energy to becoming interpersonally skilled and wise. There are things you know and things you can do that make it sometimes appear to others as if you can read minds and work magic. Indeed, you do understand aspects of effective living that remain a mystery to many others.

On the other hand, this profession offers nowhere to hide. Your worst fears are played out in sessions every day. You suffer the stresses and strains inherent to looking deeply into the core of what it means to be human—including the terrors, challenges, and torments that most people prefer to keep buried. Almost every week, if not every day, you encounter people living out the nightmares you, yourself, fear the most—addicted to drugs, out of control, mortally wounded from abuse they have suffered, depressed and suicidal, monumentally self-destructive, without hope. In addition, being a therapist forces you to examine your own motives for the choices you have made and continue to make, including the decision to be a therapist in the first place.

Why You Became a Therapist

Examining your motives for becoming a therapist is a logical place to begin this personal journey. It isn't as if you've never given the subject some thought, nor been asked to recite an appropriate, usually altruistic, set of reasons that highlight your devotion to service to humankind. Surely the allure of fame and riches weren't the big attraction; rather, most of us felt drawn to the idea that we might do some good for others—and, we hoped, for ourselves as well.

Your Hopes

When we began this journey, each of us had some fantasies about what being a therapist would be like. I pictured myself ministering to the walking wounded, healing them with a kind word or brilliant story. I hoped that my family and friends would respect what I was doing; even more important, I wished I would finally respect myself. I thought about working in the company of a dozen like-minded folks, colleagues who were wise and witty and open and caring. I imagined that I would feel good about the work I would be doing, that it would be important and valuable; it would be a true calling to which I could devote all my boundless energy.

Once upon a time, you had some definite dreams, as well hazy fantasies, about what your training would prepare you to do. List here, in no particular order, a few things you hoped to achieve by becoming a therapist.

1. Help troubled children

2. Be highly respected

3. Understand how/ why people function

4.

5.

Meeting Your Expectations

In spite of what we imagined becoming a therapist might involve and what it would do for us, such expectations were often based on misguided assumptions and inadequate information. In my own case, it turned out that I learned far more than I ever thought possible about the means by which to better understand others and myself. Many of my initial expectations were exceeded with respect to learning interpersonal skills, helping strategies, and useful ways to make sense of the world. Yet I was surprised at how little I actually learned in the classroom compared to practical experiences in the field, informal conversations with classmates and instructors, and certainly lessons from my clients. I was shocked by the hypocrisy I encountered among professionals in the field, especially among those who didn't seem to be able to practice in their own lives what they were supposedly teaching to us. Finally, I was disappointed to discover that my therapist training did not forever banish my self-doubts, as I had hoped.

Review the list you created in the previous exercise, and reflect on the items you described. Compare what you hoped would happen to what has actually taken place in your work as a therapist. For a few of the items just identified, jot down some notes to yourself about the extent to which you satisfied your expectations.

1. Helping children & families

2.

3.

In the space provided, consider which items you listed that you are not feeling especially hopeful about. Say something to yourself about how your dreams were compromised or abandoned.

Understanding how people function.

Some Personal Motives

Let's take it as a given that almost everyone in this field is, to some degree, committed to helping other people and making the world a better place. We all hoped that we could do something useful as a result of our therapist training. Perhaps we even thought that others might profit from the pain we suffered or the obstacles we faced in our lives.

It is a bit more challenging, and a lot more threatening, to examine the intensely personal and private reasons that may have led you to become a therapist. These motives were not part of your conscious hopes or your expressed expectations. Even now it is rare to hear therapists speak aloud about the personal reasons they do this sort of work—beyond, of course, their desire to help others. Nevertheless, many of us do acknowledge that being a therapist provides us with a degree of respectability, a feeling of self-efficacy, and a way of enjoying one-way intimacy in which we are the ones in control, the ones with the power.

I am reluctant to admit that I became a therapist because I hoped to reassure myself about my own emotional stability. The more clients I saw, the more convinced I became that I wasn't as crazy as I thought I was. I found that I enjoyed being the one in charge of the relationship, the one who was treated with respect, as if I really knew and understood things that, quite honestly, seemed awfully vague to me. Furthermore, I really enjoyed hearing people's stories; it satisfied my intense curiosity as a spectator. But unlike watching television, I could even tinker with the plot. And each time someone was influenced positively by my efforts, I felt redeemed, as if what I did really mattered. Because I felt so worthless early in life, to this day I don't feel totally comfortable before I fall asleep at night unless I can identify something helpful that I did for others.

In the following list of personal motives that some therapists have acknowledged, check those items that seem to fit for you:

- ☑ Need for control
- ❑ Need for power
- ☑ Observe as a spectator
- ❑ One-way intimacy
- ☑ Understand people or myself
- ❑ Become an instrument of change
- ❑ Obtain self-therapy
- ☑ Save the world
- ☑ Rescue and heal
- ❑ Be a know-it-all
- ❑ Live vicariously
- ☑ Earn prestige and respect
- ❑ Make a decent living
- ❑ Settle into a profession

These are just a few of the many possibilities that could have influenced, and may still have an impact on, your decision to be a therapist. In the space provided, speak as honestly and openly as you can about the personal motives you have for doing therapeutic work.

I agree w/ Kottler, I can use client's experiences as a measuring stick to my emotional stability.

Consequences of Being a Therapist

Our clients often come to us with wildly unrealistic expectations about what we can do to help them. They seem to think we have magic wands, that we will "cure" their spouses, banish their addictions, fix all their problems, or agree with them completely. We may find their innocence or ignorance amusing, if not counterproductive to our efforts; but at times, the hopes we held for what therapist training would do for us were no more realistic.

Regardless of the personal as well as professional motives at stake, a number of misconceptions were, and continue to be, perpetuated during training years. Only after we get into the field and spend considerable time facing the realities of therapeutic practice do we learn a number of difficult lessons for which we may have been unprepared. For example, clinical practice is not composed of a series of decision points at which there are only four choices, like a multiple-choice test, one of which is correct; nor are the answers we are searching for found in the indexes of books. Furthermore, some clients will not improve much no matter how hard we try, and some situations we will face will have no satisfactory resolutions.

In therapist training programs we often got the idea that we would have plenty of time to set up treatment plans and implement them. Little did we fully understand that, much of the time, we would be lucky to have a half-dozen sessions with a very disturbed client. Then there was all the paperwork and organizational politics, for which we may have been unprepared. Little did we realize that some of our most difficult challenges would come from dealing with our own colleagues!

Supply personal examples of the following lessons that directly con-tradict what you expected originally. Whereas some of these lessons might fit your situation, others will not; address the ones that speak most to your own experience.

- Life isn't a multiple-choice exam.

- Answers aren't found in books.

- What you do is often absurd.
  Deaf Education Teacher!

- Your family still won't listen to you.

- You will never feel good enough.

- You will never really understand how therapy works.

- This job has negative side effects.
  I carry the weight of other people's emotions.
  I feel responsible for client's progress.

- Some people don't respect what you do.
  Deaf Ed.

- Some clients don't improve no matter what you do.
  Narcassim or low IQ (London Smith)

Stages of Growth and Transformation

The unrealistic expectations and distorted hopes we held, the things we never learned in school, didn't prepare us for all the inevitable difficulties we faced along the journey. Nevertheless, by talking to more experienced colleagues, you probably learned that you weren't alone in your struggles: All therapists go through a series of stages along their journeys.

During the training years, a number of themes emerge that are quite different from those that occur during the middle career stages or the later years as a veteran and then a master practitioner. Whether you are just beginning your training in school, in your first years of practice, a veteran enjoying a sense of competence, or a mentor and supervisor for others, you experience some unique developmental challenges to remain energized and avoid burnout. Of course, most of us straddle more than one of these stages at a time.

For each of these stages that applies to you, write down one story from your own life to describe how this theme resonates with your experiences.

Training Stage: "What if I Don't Have What It Takes?"

Example: I remember sitting in my first class, looking around the room, thinking to myself that everyone else seemed so much brighter than me. Sometimes I didn't even understand the questions they asked, much less the answers that were given.

Watching the microskill videos thinking how will I internalize all these skills?

Hero Worship Stage: "If Only I Could Be Like You."

Example: Some of my professors and supervisors seemed to know and understand everything. I was in awe of the seemingly effortless way that they could get to the core of an issue and then provide an assortment of apparently brilliant interventions. They never seemed to be at a loss, and always seemed to know exactly what to do in any situation.

Enchantment Stage: "I Can't Believe I Get Paid for Doing This!"

Example: I was sitting with this one client who was so interesting, so grateful for my help, that I felt like paying *her* for the privilege of talking to her. I think I learned as much from her as she learned from me.

Competence Stage: "I Seem to Know What I'm Doing!"

Example: There came a time when I began to notice that I could anticipate what my supervisors would say to me. In fact, after a while I was using them more as a sounding board for my own ideas. Then I became aware that I was picking out a few things that even they didn't notice or understand.

(continued)

Honeymoon Stage: "Hey, I'm Really Good at This!"

Example: It's rare these days when a new client comes in that I don't feel reasonably confident that I can do something to be helpful. At least, I usually have a good idea where to start.

Midcareer Doubt Stage: "What If I'm Not Really Doing Anything?"

Example: I've been thinking a lot lately about whether my life's work really means anything, whether what I've been doing all these years really makes much of a difference. It seems as if no matter how hard I work or how much I learn, so many people I see don't have much of a chance in life.

Preburnout Stage: "Another Day, Another Dollar."

Example: This has become just a job to me. I sit with my clients, try to stay attentive most of the time, accept the limits of what I can do, and leave the rest to them. I figure, in just a few more years I can move into another job so I don't have to do this stuff anymore. It's just not the same anymore.

Revitalization Stage: "What in Me Is Getting in the Way?"

Example: I've recently experienced a rebirth of sorts. I have completely changed the way I do things. For many years I felt I'd become stale, seeing the same old clients doing pretty similar things. Now I've refashioned myself, developed a new specialty area, and started confronting more often the ways I have avoided looking at my own blocks. I've never felt more creative and excited by the work that I do.

Mentorship Stage: "You Want to Be Like Me?"

Example: I seem to have attained that place once occupied by my own mentors: Therapists now come to me for guidance. I'm not sure exactly when or how this happened, but it almost seems as if I have attained a degree of wisdom.

(continued)

Review

This chapter begins the journey by examining your initial hopes and expectations for being a therapist and comparing them to the realities of your professional practice. You looked at the stages of your growth and evolution as a practitioner, starting from where you've been and, now, heading toward the future. Beginners projected themselves into the future, while veterans looked back on their earliest years.

In reviewing the thoughts and feelings that were stirred up in you while doing the preceding reflective exercises, what one issue stands out for you, and is one that you want to hold onto?

Self-doubt is a major issue.

I cannot use the client as a measuring stick for my own mental health.

CHAPTER 2

Joys and Privileges of Therapeutic Work

It isn't just what we do as therapists that defines our work, but also our inner experiences. No matter what our setting and specific assignments, we are essentially paid to continually improve ourselves in a multitude of ways. All the books we read, the workshops we complete, the supervision sessions we attend, the conversations we have with colleagues, and especially the sessions we conduct, help us to become more highly skilled and personally effective. As we hear ourselves talk to clients, we are also speaking to ourselves. As we construct new, more creative ways to promote change in others, we cannot help but apply these lessons to our own lives.

Even with the hazards of the profession, the hardships and challenges we face, this is still the best job in the world. Who of us can possibly believe that we get to hear such interesting life stories? We are honored and privileged to be the designated healers of psychic pain in our culture. We are highly tuned instruments of compassion and caring. Sure, there are days when we seriously question our own sanity for working as hard as we do for relatively little compensation or appreciation. Yet no matter how discouraged or frustrated we might feel on any given day, it's still difficult to imagine doing anything else that provides such stimulation and satisfaction.

This chapter helps you examine exactly what you experience as most fulfilling about your work. The profile you develop will help you to identify some areas to explore further in later chapters and finally to initiate some constructive changes in the ways you function.

We'll start with the good news.

Joys and Satisfactions

In addition to asking a client what's wrong, we might also check out what is going particularly well. This allows us to start on a positive note, to assess strengths and resources, and gives us time to get warmed up before we delve into areas that are most uncomfortable.

Having worked as a teacher for a number of years, one of the things I learned quickly was to stay the heck out of the teachers' lounge during breaks. Because I was filled with excitement, it was discouraging for me to hear most of my colleagues complain constantly about how much they were unappreciated, how unmotivated their students were, and how much they looked forward to the holidays. Once I became a therapist, I observed a similar phenomenon when colleagues got together: Everyone would compete with one another over who had the most resistant clients or challenging cases. Some therapists would talk about their clients in the most derogatory manner, using terrible words to describe them, like "hateful," "borderline," or a "pain in the ass." Others would whine about "the administration" or the lack of adequate resources and salaries requisite to their own commitment. As much as I yearned for companionship, I felt increasingly dispirited hanging out with some coworkers who, basically, didn't much enjoy their work.

I'm not saying that our job isn't really, really hard. Nor am I implying that we don't have legitimate reasons to feel unappreciated or discouraged at times. Rather, I am suggesting that we don't pay nearly enough attention to the joys and benefits of what we do. In the sections to follow I suggest several aspects of therapeutic work that are especially enjoyable and stimulating, supported with a personal example. For each of them, I invite you to supply your own story of some facet that was fun, interesting, or enjoyable for you.

Personal Disclosures

I find it difficult to watch television because the stories I hear in therapy are so much more interesting; plus, I get to be part of the narrative and, at times, even direct new plotlines for the script.

People disclose confidences to us in therapy about their professions, their sex lives, and their relationships that are so incredible we can hardly keep a straight face. Every day we hear stories that are compelling, at times mind-numbing or heart-wrenching, and we can barely catch our breath between them. We are privileged (and burdened) to listen to the stories of those who are most disturbed, but also sometimes most interesting.

> Jot down here a few of the most intriguing or haunting stories that you've heard from clients, those that you will remember for a long time.

Sense of Drama and Arousal

Often related to the vicarious experiences just described are the ways that we are entertained and stimulated by the narratives we hear in therapy, incredible stories that inspire, disturb, and/or haunt us in ways that make everyday conversations pale by comparison. I don't know about you, but I have been spoiled by the intense, moving, raw dramas that unfold in sessions with my clients. Sure, there is sometimes a kind of "secondary trauma" or "compassion fatigue" that results from getting so close to the flame of others' misery or self-destructive behavior; at the same time, there is often a tremendous joy and excitement that results from hearing stories that may have never been shared with anyone before.

I have, for example, heard about the depth of deprivation among sex workers, about the most perverse sexual behavior imaginable; likewise, I have been privy to the inner workings of politics, the lifestyles of writers and actors, even the best ways for a hired killer to hide bodies so they won't be discovered. I have learned what it is like to be blind, deaf, paralyzed, or irreparably wounded by childhood abuse. I have talked with serial killers on death row and with Buddhist nuns who minister to the dying. In short, I have lived ten thousand lives through the stories of my clients. I have visited heaven with some of them; also, hell.

Rather than relating a representative story you've heard that focuses on the tragedy of a human life, describe a dramatic story you've been privileged to hear that inspires you in some way.

Making a Difference

I sometimes pinch myself that I have the opportunity to make a small difference in the world. There is a saying from the Talmud that by saving one life, we save the world. I believe that to be utterly true. We give meaning to our lives through service to others. Whatever suffering we once experienced is now useful to help others through similar troubles. In some small way, as a result of our presence on this planet, we are helping to reduce misery and guide others to enjoy more fulfilling and productive lives. Incredible, isn't it?

As I write these words, I am still feeling tearful about a young girl I encountered while working in a remote village in Nepal. She was cold, so I offered her my jacket, which she refused. It was then that I noticed her face was swollen, the result of an infection that if left untreated, I later learned, might disfigure or even kill her. I arranged for her to see a doctor and receive antibiotics, for less than cost of a meal. I realize that in doing therapy we rarely get the opportunity to help someone in such a direct and decisive way, but this incident nevertheless reminded me about the satisfaction I get—a "helper's high," if you will—from making a positive difference in someone's life.

Share one memorable example of something you did or said that made a significant difference in someone's life, one that neither you nor he or she will ever forget.

Helping the middle schoolers accept their deafness & embrace deaf culture

Taylor Carter.

Intimacy

Quick: Think of a helping relationship that immediately comes to mind that seems almost transcendent in the caring, empathy, closeness, even mutual "love" that was felt and experienced.

Describe that relationship here, as well as the feelings of caring and intimacy that you experienced.

The Therapist's Workbook

What comes to mind for me when I ask myself the same question is a rather frustrating encounter with a difficult adolescent girl who refused to speak or even acknowledge my presence in the room. Her sadness and despair was so profound that I could barely sit with her, especially because of the helplessness I felt to do anything to alleviate her pain; she only seemed to be getting worse. She punished me with her silence—or so it felt at the time. In truth, she was just so filled with anguish she could barely hold herself together. I have never felt more impotent and worthless.

As is often the case, it took time for us to develop trust and to learn about one another. I don't wish to gloss over how difficult these many months were—for both of us. But eventually we reached an accommodation of sorts, although it remained awkward and uncomfortable. This was one of the most challenging cases I've ever worked on, not just because this child's symptoms were so intractable, but because I so badly wanted to know her and wanted her to know me. Perhaps it was because the journey was so difficult and painful for both of us that the intimacy that ultimately emerged was that much more satisfying and memorable.

Growth and Learning

What did you learn this week?

How many jobs do you know in which even after years of practice, decades of devotion to the craft, you still learn new things on a regular basis, about the work, about the world, about others—and most of all, about *yourself*? If you really pay attention to what is going on in your sessions with clients, if you maintain a mindful, hovering awareness, a day won't go by that you don't learn something new—sometimes even have an insight that is life-altering.

This week I sat with a group of adolescent girls, listening to their life stories, which are very difficult. Most are victims of poverty and extreme neglect; some have been abused. Yet they are incredibly resilient and hopeful for the future. I wondered: How can children who have so little, who have suffered so much, remain so upbeat about what is possible? In contrast, I realized, I enjoy so many privileges and advantages, and still it is never enough. I'm always thinking about what's next. I am still driven by ambition and a desire for more of whatever it is I have. I spend money without concern about whether I actually need what I purchase. I complain about things that frustrate me. I have never learned the patience that I see in these girls' eyes. I admire and respect them for a kind of strength I fear I will never achieve. They inspire me to try harder to seek balance in my life. They motivate me to try to do more to help those who are dramatically disadvantaged. Finally, they help me to confront my shame about my own limitations.

Now it's your turn. First, share something significant that you learned this week (or month) from your work, something that has the potential to alter the trajectory of your life.

You can't help everyone
↳ save

The Therapist's Workbook

What resolution or commitment would you be prepared to make in order to become more mindful of the ways you grow as a result of your therapeutic work?

To be aware of compassion fatigue & find ways to prevent it.

Playing Detective

Being a therapist is not only about emotional activation but also intellectual challenges. We are practical philosophers, deputized to make sense of life's mysteries and solve puzzles that seem to be missing critical pieces. Even for those who work in an action-oriented style, who either don't have the interest or the time to deal much with insight, there are still interesting and complex phenomena to decode, or the need to make connections between seemingly unrelated actions or events.

There are always questions that come up in sessions, if not in our own minds, when trying to sort out diagnostic issues and construct appropriate interventions. We are detectives in this way, looking for clues as to why the problems or symptoms are making their presence known at this particular time. We wonder what functions or purposes are being served by the difficulties. We explore the particular meanings of the issues within the context of the client's life. We are often called upon to help people make sense of their lives and discover deeper meaning in their actions and choices. We are asked to uncover the ways life narratives are often shaped by one's culture, gender, and other dimensions. We examine issues of power in human relationships, as well as systemic influences that both exacerbate problems as well as potentially heal them.

In a multitude of other ways, we essentially help people to make greater sense of what is going on in their lives, not because it is always required to produce lasting changes, but because it can be so satisfying to do so. And all the while we are acting as "meaning-makers" for our clients, we cannot help but be doing so in our own lives, asking ourselves how whatever is going on with them relates directly to some aspect of our own unresolved issues.

> Regardless of your preferred theoretical orientation and clinical style, list ways that you act as a detective in your work with clients, facilitating greater self-awareness and deeper understanding.
>
> Pay attention to affect, & body language & what the client isn't saying.

I work a lot in other cultures, where I am expected to have a high level of understanding about the local rituals, customs, and practices. Needless to say, I am often confused, even at a loss, about what is really going on much of the time, a predicament that produces a lot of anxiety and fear that I will do or say something spectacularly stupid or inappropriate.

Recently, I felt both frustrated and stuck about why I wasn't making much progress with an individual who was a critical power player in changes we were structuring within his community. I tried everything I could think of to appease this elder, but all my efforts only seemed to make things worse. Logic seemed to be of little use in solving this mystery, so I was forced to rely more on inductive and intuitive processes. My (or I should say *our*) breakthrough occurred only after I abandoned what I thought I knew and understood and instead accepted that I was completely ignorant in the circumstance. Thus, instead of taking on the role of Sherlock Holmes to break the impasse, I adopted the position of an innocent child. This produced a greater sense of humility, one of "not knowing," that allowed me to see, feel, and sense some aspects of the situation that had previously been hidden from view.

> Reflecting back on recent sessions with your clients, describe an example of an interesting insight that emerged, one that required both a degree of intuition as well as intellectual rigor on your part to generate.

As a way to review the best aspects of your work as a therapist, it is periodically useful to assess your levels of satisfaction in areas that matter the most to you. Use the instrument provided to summarize some of the joys, satisfactions, and privileges you experience as a therapist.

Rate Your Satisfaction

Rate on a scale of 5 (very important) to 1 (not important at all) how meaningful the following items are to your satisfaction in this work.

Very Important (5)	Important (4)	Moderately Important (3)	Relatively Unimportant (2)	Not Important At All (1)

Item	Description	Rating
Spectator	Having access to the private lives of others.	5 4 ③ 2 1
Altruism	Feeling as though I am making a difference in someone's life.	⑤ 4 3 2 1
Control	Gaining a sense of power or potency in knowing or doing things.	5 ④ 3 2 1
Intimacy	Enjoying close connections.	5 4 ③ 2 1
Learning	Accumulating knowledge about the world and human behavior.	⑤ 4 3 2 1
Growth	Being challenged and stimulated to confront my own unresolved issues.	5 ④ 3 2 1
Creativity	Devising new ways of making sense of complex issues.	5 ④ 3 2 1
Drama	Enjoying the excitement and intensity of therapeutic encounters.	5 4 ③ 2 1
Narratives	Being captivated by the human stories shared in sessions.	⑤ 4 3 2 1
Arousal	Getting caught up in the intensity of feelings expressed.	5 4 ③ 2 1
Mentoring	Being part of someone's journey toward growth and change.	⑤ 4 3 2 1
Curiosity	Following clues and unraveling mysteries underlying client issues.	⑤ 4 3 2 1
Challenge	Matching wits with people who are resistant.	⑤ 4 3 2 1
Reflection	Being contemplative, analytical, and/or intuitive as a lifestyle.	5 ④ 3 2 1

Reflection on Joys and Satisfactions

Now that you've rated the items in the table, make a list of the joys that stand out for you in being a therapist. Feel free to add others that weren't included.

Altruism
Control
Learning
Growth
Creativity
Narratives
Mentoring
Curiosity
challenge
Reflection

Check It Out and Report Back

Keep the list of joys and satisfactions with you in your wallet or purse, adding other aspects of the work that you especially prize as time goes on. Spend one complete week taking inventory of all the things you truly love about being a therapist.

Sometime, when you are sitting around with colleagues, review your list with them. Ask them to brainstorm with you other joys and satisfactions they associate with being a therapist. Add here a few of their ideas that resonate with you.

1.

2.

(continued)

3.

4.

5.

There is little doubt that therapeutic work is among the most challenging, stressful, emotionally arousing, and difficult professions, especially because we spend time with people when they are desperate and often displaying their worst behavior. Although we will spend plenty of time in the next and other chapters exploring some of these hardships, it is also important to honor the amazing gifts we receive as a result of our commitment to helping others. We learn so much every day—about our clients, about people in general, about ourselves, and about the way the world works. We are privy to the deepest secrets that people rarely share with anyone else. We enjoy levels of intimacy and trust in relationships that are unprecedented in almost any other context. And we are privileged to accompany individuals on their journeys of redemption during their most difficult times.

CHAPTER 3

Identifying Sources of Stress

If the good news is that you enjoy quite a few benefits as a result of being a therapist, the bad news is you also pay a dear price for them. Being a therapist is hard, hard work, sometimes both emotionally and physically exhausting. Each day, we sit in a sanctuary where people file in and dump their problems, share their suffering, play defensive games, test the limits of what they can get away with, and sometimes do whatever they can to earn their reputations as incorrigible or hopeless cases. At times, it feels like we are sentenced to join them in a psychological prison, with no chance of parole.

Over time you may begin to experience a number of symptoms and side effects of your work, running the gambit from forms of self-medication and acting-out behavior to unhealthy lifestyle choices. The same symptoms of stress that afflict your clients—discouragement, frustration, disengagement, boredom, depression, and burnout—may strike you as well, especially after years of practice.

This is a big chapter, as it should be, for it covers a critical path along this journey. It will take courage, a willingness to take risks, and fortitude to be really honest with yourself about the issues that plague you the most, and to face the weaknesses that compromise your personal and professional effectiveness.

Fair warning: The exercises contained herein are specifically designed to stir things up a bit.

Sources of Stress in a Therapist's Life

The process we often follow with our clients begins with a description of presenting issues and identification of contributing undercurrents. Next, some attention is often devoted to exploring the factors that contribute most to the disturbing symptoms. It is no less valid to apply this same process to the life of a therapist.

(margin note, handwritten, rotated: Compassion fatigue)

While some of us experience a kind of chronic angst that is triggered by getting too close to other people's pain, all of us, at times, feel a degree of stress from the inevitable challenges that come with the job. We live with pressure brought on by work settings—the politics, paperwork, and time demands that require more from us than we can possibly deliver. There are also unrealistic demands placed on us by clients—that we fix them in a single meeting, that we suffer their verbal abuse, that we tolerate their acting out. Another source of stress emanates from events in our lives, some of them normal developmental transitions like those of our clients, others brought on by life crises related to loss and death, family conflicts, financial problems, or physical maladies. Finally, there is the anxiety we bring on ourselves through our own feelings of perfectionism and/or self-doubt. Although not all these forms of stress may be a problem for you, it's likely that at least a few of them will hit home as you read.

As you review the following inventory of contributors to stress, identify any that seem particularly relevant to your life. Write an explanatory note to yourself next to those items that seem especially troublesome.

Client-Induced Stress

This category of stress results from client behavior, especially when acting out takes place, we experience some sort of extreme abuse, or we become a pawn in, for example, the power games of a toxic family.

Perhaps like you, I have had clients manipulate me for their own nefarious ends. I have been told whopper lies—I mean complete fabrications. I have been screamed at for failing to meet expectations; I have been triangulated into dysfunctional systemic dynamics; I have watched clients deteriorate no matter what I tried to do. I have, variously, felt helpless, incompetent, or discouraged, and have lost faith in my helping powers along the way.

Check any of the following that have recently been part of your client experiences. Elaborate on those that have been most distressing to you.

- ❏ Client's angry outbursts
- ❏ Accusations of incompetence
- ❏ Client's intense depression and lethargy
- ❏ Presentation of truly overwhelming problems (e.g., incest, incredible deprivation, terrible loss, and so on)
- ❏ Suicidal threats
- ❏ Triangulation into client's family
- ❏ Client's deceit or lies
- ❏ Premature termination
- ❏ Client's major deterioration

Work Environment Stress

This group of stress precipitants is related to the work setting in which you practice. Perhaps the demands of your job, the behavior of your colleagues and/or supervisors, the bureaucracy of your organization, or the requirements of managed care operations handicap you in ways that make it difficult for you to recover and remain focused and productive.

Begin by checking all the work environment stressors that apply.

- ☐ Time pressures
- ☑ Caseload that is excessive in size, scope, or intensity
- ☑ Organizational politics
- ☐ Rules and restrictions on freedom
- ☐ Unsupportive or difficult colleagues
- ☑ Supervisory incompetence
- ☑ Excessive paperwork
- ☐ Unrealistic or unreasonable demands by organization or managed care
- ☐ Torn allegiances between client, organization, and self
- ☑ Lack of money or resources

Now describe examples of those that have been most difficult for you to manage, and why.

Larry Williams – Deaf Ed – Crowley ISD
Sped paper work
underpaid teacher

Event-Related Stress

The first two sets of stressors are related to factors mostly associated with other people's behavior; this category and the next one are connected more to your own attitudes or actions.

The first group results from experiences in your personal life that may affect how you perform on the job.

How many of these apply to you?

- ☐ Legal actions taken against you
- ☑ Major life transitions (age transitions and developmental changes)
- ☑ Traumas from the past
- ☐ Life crises
- ☑ Physical or medical problems
- ☑ Family problems
- ☑ Economic cutbacks
- ☑ Money pressures
- ☑ Change in job responsibilities

Write about those that are currently causing the most difficulties for you.

Medical problems/bills
PTSD
Mother/Daughter relationship
Job search

(continued)

Self-Induced Stress

The last set of stressors are all self-initiated, as a result of unrealistic expectations, faulty thinking, or unresolved personal issues that interfere with your ability to accept or forgive yourself for your limitations.

Check all that resonate for you.

- ☑ Feelings of perfectionism
- ☑ Fear of failure
- ☐ Self-doubt
- ☑ Need for approval
- ☑ Emotional depletion
- ☐ Unhealthy lifestyle

Now, look back and try to see the pattern that emerges, and note which items seem to have the greatest impact on your stress levels.

Perfectionism
feel of failure

Sources of Stress from Clinical Work

Although the nature of your job, the people you work with, and the settings you work in impose some of the stress in your life, pressure also emanates from the particular strengths and weaknesses of your clinical style. As hard as you try to be helpful to your clients, you face personal and professional limitations on a daily basis. Furthermore, you confront your own lapses in knowledge, execution, and thinking. There isn't a session you've ever conducted about which you can't think of at least a dozen things you could have done differently or of a few issues that you wished you had handled in another way.

Self-Assessment: Weaknesses

Since your earliest training, what weaknesses in your clinical work have been most consistently identified by supervisors? List several in each category (resist the urge to skip any).

Case Conceptualization

The particular formulation of treatment plans often includes consistent lapses or errors that result from our blind spots and biases.

Example: "I consistently fail to recognize cultural and gender differences in client narratives, relying too much on what is familiar and what I assume, based on my own prior experience."

Personal Characteristics

Therapeutic effectiveness results not only from the mastery of skills and therapeutic interventions but also from personal qualities.

Example: "My need to be right interferes with my flexibility to try alternative strategies."

Right-Fighter

(continued)

Attitudes

If I were to interview your former clients, what would they tell me are some of your most prominent attitudes and beliefs that you think you were able to control or disguise?

   Example: "Some clients sense my unflattering judgment of them because I think they are not as ambitious and productive as they could or should be."

Clinical Skills

We learned a number of identifiable generic therapeutic skills in training: interpretation, confrontation, reflection of feeling, goal setting, and so on. It is likely that you execute certain of these skills better than others. What are some of your particular weaknesses?

   Example: "I confront prematurely and, when facing resistance, press onward stubbornly."

Managing Boundaries

To what extent are you able to deal appropriately and consistently with boundary issues?

Example: "Previous problems with authority figures interfere with my willingness to enforce consistent limits with clients who test me."

Clients from Hell

During a time in my life when I was "toast"—totally burned out by my work—I had this great idea for a book that I would call *Clients from Hell*. Each chapter would be about a specific kind of client that seemed to me had been sent from hell to make my life miserable. There was the adolescent who would tell me to "go fuck myself"; the client who wouldn't talk; the one who rambled constantly; the one who dutifully came to sessions but never made any progress; the client who continuously lied; the one who was manipulative, controlling, noncompliant, resistant, challenging, abusive; and so on. I think you get the idea.

One of the reviewers of the book suggested I might have a problem in that I seemed to have lost my compassion.

Bingo!

Describe the clients who most often and successfully get under your skin and who seem to you have been "sent from hell" to torture you and shatter any illusions you may have that you know what you're doing.

People who are condescending or entitled

(continued)

Guiding into the Unknown

We therapists can sometimes get in a rut, where we prefer to stick with what is familiar and comfortable rather than venturing into new territory that carries certain risks. Just like our clients, we may be reluctant to take risks—for example, trying creative innovations that might not work out as anticipated, even though the situation might require such new explorations.

When have you gotten stuck in a rut and failed to take "the road less traveled"?

Example: "I rely way too much on the same old metaphors, stories, and favorite interventions because it feels like too much work to adapt, create, or discover strategies that are better customized to each client and situation."

Living with Confusion and Uncertainty

Let's be honest: Some of the time we have no idea what is really going on with a client or during a session. One of the major life tasks of a therapist is to learn to tolerate this confusion and uncertainty, even embrace the mysterious nature of human experience.

> How has being unable or unwilling to live with confusion and uncertainty impacted your therapeutic practice?
>
> Example: "I became a therapist in the first place because I wanted the illusion of certainty, truth, and understanding. I wanted to simplify the complexity and ambiguity of my life. I still struggle with honoring the mysteries of life and the complexity of human behavior without the need to reduce them to simple (albeit, faulty) assumptions."

agree
Not knowing bothers me but God will reveal his plan in time

Remaining Fully Present

What percentage of the time in sessions would you estimate that you are truly and completely present? I have been asking this question of hundreds of therapists over the years, curious about what they would say. I have heard estimates ranging from one-quarter to three-quarters of the time—although I think even 50 percent is overstating, especially with some individuals.

Of course, there are some clients to whom we remain riveted almost all the time because their stories are so compelling or because we are so engaged in the relationship. Then there are the others, for whom we are barely present; we "check out," just nodding from time to time and glancing at the clock every few minutes, amazed so little time has elapsed.

What about you? What percentage of the time would you estimate you remain truly engaged in the sessions with a typical client?

Example: "This is a tough one for me! As much as I concentrate, as hard as I try to remain focused, my attention constantly wanders. I feel itchy sitting still for long periods of time. I become bored easily. I want to be entertained by my clients, and tune out when I think I've heard it all before."

This is my fear, but even w/ students I am approx. 75-85% focused b/c I am alway trying to find more clues into their background & understanding.

Even more interesting, when you "leave the room," when your attention wanders, where do you go? What are your favorite escape fantasies, and what do you think they say about you?

Sometimes book I'm reading or something I recently learned.

Self-Assessment: Strengths

You've reviewed your weaknesses and limitations in the areas examined in this section. Now it's time to record your greatest strengths in each.

Case Conceptualization

Personal Characteristics

Attitudes

Clinical Skills

(continued)

Managing Boundaries

To expand this exercise, consult with at least two other colleagues who are intimately familiar with your clinical work and ask them what they see as your greatest gifts as a therapist. Note here what you learned from them and then compare this information with your own self-assessment.

Assessing the Hazards

As we've been discussing, therapists experience a number of side effects from and suffer hazards in their work. Some of the most commonly reported are listed in the next exercise for you to evaluate.

The Therapist's Workbook

Hazard Assessment

Rate these hazards on a scale of 1 to 3, being as honest as you can with yourself about the extent to which each of them is or may be a problem for you. If you sense that you may be denying or disowning some of these issues, discuss them with others you know well and trust to be truthful.

Hazard Rating Scale

Not a problem: 1

Could be a problem: 2

Definitely a problem: 3

Common Hazardous Attitudes

_2_ Arrogance: I am perceived by others as a know-it-all.

_1_ Omnipotence: I inflate my sense of power and control.

_2_ Cynicism: I act as though I've seen it all, and I appear skeptical.

_1_ Narcissism: I take myself too seriously and/or inflate my self-importance.

_1_ Hypocrisy: I don't practice in my own life what I expect of others.

Comment: In the teaching community I am def. a cynic.

Self-Defeating Work Habits

_3_ Workaholism: I work too many hours and overstructure my life.

_1_ Negligence: I act out by failing to complete paperwork in a timely manner.

_1_ Boredom: I feel bored and stale in sessions, like I'm going through the motions.

_3_ Isolation: I spend too much time alone.

(continued)

_____1_____ Unidimensionality: I hang around only with other therapists and talk about work-related stuff.

Comment:

For sure am a workaholic & I prefer to be alone to avoid unwanted drama or gossip.

Other Side Effects

_____2_____ Futility: I get discouraged and frustrated with progress (or lack thereof) in my work.

_____2_____ Fatigue: I lead a lifestyle that drains me of energy.

_____1_____ Intellectualizing: I restrict my degree of emotional expressiveness.

_____2_____ Mistrust: I find it difficult to experience intimacy in my personal relationships.

_____1_____ Relationships: I face a number of conflicts with colleagues at work.

Comment:

I have extremely high expect. of myself

My health & compassion drain me.

Formulating a Self-Diagnosis

Now that you have completed the hazard assessment "intake questionnaire," along with the exercises earlier in the chapter, create a kind of diagnostic impression of yourself based on the data generated. I am not talking about choosing a label from the *DSM*, but rather about writing a summary case report, describing yourself as if you were a client who walked into your own office.

For example, I might write about myself as follows:

> This is an individual with a high level of need for approval, which he can't seem to satisfy. He reports that his ambition and drive to succeed seem out of control, to the point where he is often planning for the future rather than enjoying the present. He appears to struggle with boredom a lot, stirring things up in his life periodically as a way to meet his need for novelty and stimulation. Although he says that he wants more intimate friendships in his life, he reports that he has not been successful in making that happen to the extent he'd like. Issues of power and control, two main themes in his life, might interfere with his ability and willingness to compromise in relationships.

Write a similar case report and diagnostic impression of your own patterns.

This individual is highly perfectionist and guarded. She reports the need to always keep busy or she'll lose her mind.

Looking at Relationships

Of the side effects you might experience as a therapist, usually those that are most problematic are related to connections to loved ones (or perhaps to the lack of such connections). Therapists are used to a high degree of intimacy, as well as conflict, in client relationships. For better or worse, this can predispose us to respond to family, friends, and colleagues in ways that are less than constructive. Conversely, there is nobody walking around this planet better equipped than a therapist to enjoy close connections with others.

Relationship Inventory

Take an inventory of your current primary relationships, noting sources of both joy and hardship. Answer the following questions by writing down the name of the person (or persons) that immediately comes to mind.

- Who is the greatest source of conflict in your personal life right now?

  Momma

- Whom do you feel most distrustful of, judged by, and in conflict with at work?

- Which of your client relationships currently feels most frustrating and futile?

Working on a Relationship

Now select one of the relationships you identified as most disturbing and disruptive in your life, and highlight what it is about this relationship that challenges you the most.

Momma- how she communicates in anger.

Next calculate the amount of time and energy you invest thinking (even obsessing) about this conflicted relationship. Describe the toll it has taken on your life.

Almost 24/7. She lives w/me.

Doing Things Differently

I don't know about you, but I hate it when I'm asked, or when I ask it of myself, what I would say to one of my clients when confronting a problem of my own. I feel like a hypocrite, certainly; but more than that, it reminds me what it feels like to be someone who may well understand what is going on but still feel powerless to change. Nevertheless, it is a good exercise.

Although there will be time in later chapters to return to this relationship problem and work out a plan for altering dysfunctional patterns, for now consider what you would say to a client who can't think of a viable way to do things differently.

Think o/side of the box.

Therapist Impairment

Take a deep breath. We are about to delve into an area that is often perceived as the most difficult for therapists to examine honestly. You would certainly not ask your clients about these issues before establishing a fairly solid relationship. And we've only just begun this journey together.

"Impairment" is an awfully strong word to use when describing any person's functioning, especially when that person is a therapist. Most of us have learned quite well from our training and have been able to shore up our defenses. We are an adaptable group, by and large. Typically, we are also good at presenting ourselves to others in the best possible light. This posture is, in fact, necessary to instill in others confidence and trust in us.

Nevertheless, for many of us the question is not *whether* we are impaired but *to what extent* we are impaired at this moment. Each of us struggles on a daily basis with our own unresolved issues that may or may not interfere with our personal and professional functioning. I am not talking here about only gross dysfunctions, such as addiction, depression, or personality disorders.

Rather, in this context, I'm defining *impairment* as any of your qualities, behaviors, or attitudes that somehow compromise your maximum effectiveness—as a human being and as a professional.

Each of us is haunted by the past. We all have unresolved issues. Most of us walk around feeling wounded at least some of the time, though we do our best to behave as if everything is just fine. But I'd like you to let the veil down for a few minutes to complete the next exercise. After all, it's just the two of us talking here.

For as many of the following questions as you like (or maybe don't like), write down what immediately comes to mind. Don't think or analyze too much; just put down the first thing that you think of. (Note: The examples following each question are intended to expand rather than limit your responses.)

- What haunts you?

    Example: "I am plagued by the feeling of not being good enough, that no matter how hard I try and how much I learn and grow, it still isn't enough for me to overcome my essential mediocrity."

    Justyn Bayer incident

- In what ways are you not fully functioning?

    Example: "I worry too much about things I can't control. I don't sleep well some nights, while my brain runs over all the things I have to do, want to do, or should do."

    - I don't sleep enough
    - constant pain

(continued)

- What are some aspects of your lifestyle that are unhealthy?

    Example: "I try to pack too much into each day, so I don't get as much time as I need to relax, to reflect on things, to enjoy more fully what I'm doing."

    - Lack of sleep
    - Dental hygiene
    - Not eating full meals

- How do you "medicate" yourself?

    Example: "That's an easy one: ice cream, or when I'm "good," frozen yogurt. That's my comfort food, the indulgence that I use instead of alcohol or drugs. I also exercise a bit too fanatically to work off excess nervous energy."

    - Sleep
    - Work

- What lies do you tell yourself?

    Example: "I say things in sessions that I convince myself are to help the client, but they are really to meet my own needs or satisfy my curiosity. I tell myself that I'm in this field primarily to help people, but I acknowledge I'm also in it for the fame and glory."

    - I'm a good person

- What are you hiding from?

    Example: "From stillness. If I stopped moving, stopped working so hard, stopped achieving, ceased all the distractions in my life, I'd face that person that is me, stripped of all adornments."

    — Lonliness
    — Stillness
    — Boredom

- How does your narcissism reveal itself?

    Example: "In my desire to be the center of attention. In the credit I seek for being the impetus, if not the motivation, for other people's growth."

    — know-it-all

- Who "gets to you" most, and why?

    Example: "Any one from whom I can sense judgment or disapproval of me. People who are bullies. People who talk in movies. People who talk loudly on their cell phones or text in the middle of a conversation. As for the why, I think it's about feeling not in control or not valued."

    - Condescending people
    - Bullies
    - Injustice
    - Unfairness   > social issues
    - Ignorance
    - Racism
    - piety

(continued)

- What is it about these questions that you find most threatening?

  Example: "That I'll have to face the fact that I don't know myself nearly as well as I pretend to, or think I do."

  I will have to deal w/ the PTSD

Looking Back

As I explained at the beginning, the purpose of this chapter was to generate as much material as possible to help us work together effectively in the exercises to come in the following chapters.

In the first go-round you might not have been as honest or forthcoming as you could have been, so before moving on to the next chapter, review your responses (or lack thereof) to the preceding exercises and note here what is haunting you the most.

the need to always be doing something; the inability to relax.

CHAPTER 4

Acknowledging Doubts, Limitations, and Failures

No matter how much preparation you do, how much training and supervision you complete, and how assiduously you address countertransference issues, failures will occur. You will fail your clients and, at times, yourself. The question is not if you will fail in your efforts to be helpful, but when you will fail next.

Certainly, not everyone subscribes to the belief that failure is an inevitable, if not necessary, part of a therapist's job. Some practitioners do not acknowledge failure as a legitimate concept; instead, they prefer to think of success in relative terms or in terms of errors and misjudgments, rather than outright failure; or they evaluate change as a series of incremental, even tiny, steps that sometimes don't seem apparent to others. Then there are clinicians who may agree that failure is a possibility, but only for others. They deny that negative outcomes may result from their own inadequacies, misjudgments, or mistakes, choosing instead to see such outcomes as the consequences of the client's poor motivation or resistance.

Regardless of how you view failure in your life and work, there is little doubt that most of us have, at one time or another, been spectacularly ill prepared to deal with our own limitations. We were taught to deny or hide our mistakes. Many of our teachers, mentors, workshop leaders, and favorite authors seemed more intent on promoting their pet theories and lauding their advantages, as opposed to talking realistically about their limitations. I can't recall the last time I went to a workshop in which I saw a video demonstration of the technique under discussion failing miserably. But that's exactly what sometimes happens for me when I take the information back to my practice, The conclusion I've inevitably reached is that it must be me who is inept because the inventors of this or that strategy acted as if it was the next foolproof miracle cure.

In supervision sessions and staff meetings as well, participants may spend more time trying to look good in front of their peers, showing off what they know, rather than discussing cases about which they genuinely feel stumped. The term *failure*, or even *mistake*, is almost never used in progress notes, and is just as rarely spoken aloud, except among one's closest confidants.

Many of us live with our doubts and sometimes feel like frauds, perpetrating the myth that we are infallible. Not all therapists suffer from internal angst and doubts, of course, but they do experience genuine, appropriate stress, caused by the brutal problems they face. In any case, there is always more that we can do to "immunize" ourselves against the inevitable disappointments we encounter.

The questions in the first exercise were exactly the ones a colleague and I asked a group of eminent therapists.

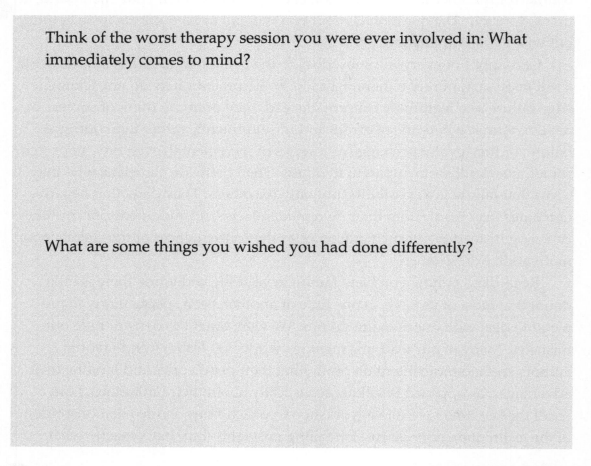

Think of the worst therapy session you were ever involved in: What immediately comes to mind?

What are some things you wished you had done differently?

What did you learn from this experience?

For most of my career I've felt utterly frustrated; I've been carrying around my deep, dark secret that my therapy doesn't look anything like the demonstrations I have seen in training videos. It's not that I'm inept at what I do, but rather that my sessions are often awkward, confusing, even chaotic at times. In addition, unlike the workshop presenters and book authors who present case after case of spectacular cures, I sometimes fail miserably—or at least my clients don't always improve as much as either of us would like.

Time after time I've attended workshops, read books, and watched videos in which the therapist appears to effortlessly and magically cure a client in a single session or two by using the prescribed treatment he or she was promoting. Yet when I would introduce the method into my own practice, it would proceed nothing like what I was led to expect. The inescapable conclusion I always came to is that I was the problem, since the technique or strategy was supposed to be foolproof.

It wasn't until I was asked to record such a training video myself that I decided it would be most productive to use the worst of the three sessions we completed instead of the best one—and it was a doozy. I wanted audiences to see what therapy really looks like. (The reason that three different clients were brought in for each demonstration was to make sure that one was usable. "You should see some of the outtakes," Jon, the producer whispered. "You wouldn't believe how hilarious they are.")

The session I chose was with a reluctant adolescent boy who had trust issues (not to mention a studio audience and three cameras running). The producer, unfortunately, denied my request to use it as the preferred

What Is Bad Therapy?

One of the first questions we asked our identified group of eminent practitioners was how they defined bad therapy. We thought we'd get a pretty clear consensus, so I was surprised at the number of different definitions supplied.

From the list of answers we collected, which do *you* think most clearly constitutes bad therapy?

- When the client becomes worse
- When the client doesn't feel heard or understood
- When the therapist feels incompetent
- When the therapist loses control
- When the therapist has no clear plan or agenda
- When the therapist repeats the same mistakes over and over
- When the therapist is arrogant or overconfident
- When there is a weak therapeutic alliance
- When the changes made don't last beyond the end of sessions

Obviously, the items on this list are not mutually exclusive. Nevertheless, I was surprised by the split between those theorists who defined bad therapy in terms of how they felt, versus the ultimate outcome for the client.

demonstration, but I learned one important thing during the filming: that most of my heroes in the field were, in fact, not necessarily competent clinicians. They might be great thinkers and writers, but many of them were not nearly as skilled at actually treating their clients.

I couldn't get Jon to agree to make a film of "bloopers" by famous therapists, but we did conspire to invite these clinicians to tell their own stories of doing really bad therapy. I figured if we could get them to admit they weren't perfect, that they failed on occasion, then maybe that would make things easier for the rest of us mortals to talk about our own imperfections and mistakes.

There are times when the client may appear to make steady progress, yet you don't feel good about the way things are proceeding; and there are other instances when you don't feel good at all about the progress, yet the client is perfectly satisfied. Likewise, a client could leave after one session and never return because he or she already got what was desired. Other situations may involve a client who is content to attend sessions regularly for years and never make a single, observable change.

I recall what I consider the single worst therapy I've ever done, with a woman I saw for several months. She used to occupy the client chair and talk incessantly without a break, often rambling on and on, repeating stories I'd heard several times previously. It did no good for me to offer any responses because she never listened. After awhile I just surrendered and sat in my chair enduring the sessions, no longer really listening to her. It never seemed to make any difference, because she barely noticed I was in the room. I had fantasies of leaving the room and returning an hour later, knowing she'd hardly miss me. I felt totally useless and, even worse, completely bored and disengaged. Here's the worst part: Even though I was doing absolutely nothing except, essentially, renting her a chair, her family continuously reported that she was improving significantly. They thought I was a miracle worker. Even more strangely, the client herself believed me to be an absolutely a brilliant therapist. How embarrassing! This was the worst failure I'd ever experienced, and yet the client was getting better, seemingly in spite of me.

In other words, bad therapy isn't as simple to identify as I originally thought. I think it's safe, however, to define it operationally as those situations when both the therapist and the client are not satisfied with the result. Once it is agreed that negative outcomes do, in fact, occur—and on a regular basis (estimated to be 10 to 20 percent of the time)—it is important to be honest with ourselves when things are not going well. This is particularly important with very difficult cases such as traumatic stress, dissociative disorders, and certain intractable conditions for which the failure rate is considerably higher.

Clients Disowning Failure

There are a number of ways therapists attempt to disown and avoid failure. It might be interesting, if not enlightening, to consider your own defensive maneuvers.

For as many of the following strategies as possible, think of examples in which you tried to distance yourself from your failures.

- *Define failure as success*: Although it's clear that your client is not improving significantly, you try to convince him or her, and yourself, that things are going far better than they really are.

- *Act as though you have everything under control*: In truth, you feel lost and confused. You don't understand what's going on and you don't have a clear idea about where to go next. Nevertheless, you act as though you are well in charge of matters.

  London Smith

- *Blame factors outside of your control*: It can't be your fault that therapy isn't working well. It must be that the client is withholding something, the client's family is sabotaging treatment, the "system" is undermining your efforts, or, simply, you're being dealt bad breaks.

  also, London Smith

You Couldn't Help

Among the greatest sources of stress in our lives as therapists are those clients we couldn't help or for whom we couldn't do enough. Perhaps there are even those who got under our skin, for reasons related to our own need for control.

In spite of my best efforts to let go of the past, accept my limitations, acknowledge my mistakes, and move forward, I am still haunted by the people I couldn't help. Maybe it was because of my poor judgment or flawed execution. More than likely, the client's own motivation and defenses played a part. Nevertheless, I can still see vividly the anguished, disappointed faces of several individuals I couldn't help.

More than a few therapists have left the field because they could not forgive themselves for a client's suicide or other self-destructive acts. Others limp along cautiously after a treatment failure, licking their wounds and taking things far too personally. In time, they may forgive themselves (assuming that forgiveness is indicated), but they will never forget. Even those clinicians who are highly skilled at accepting the limits of what they can do, who easily reframe failure as an opportunity for learning, who place primary responsibility for progress on the client's shoulders, may still feel haunted by a client or two who visited them when their guard was down.

Who Haunts You?

As you think about the helping efforts you've made throughout your life, which client haunts you the most? Which one invades your sleep or creeps into your consciousness when you least expect it? Who is the client who gets to you the most?

1. Bring to mind an image of this person.
2. Picture this person wearing an article of clothing that you associate with him or her.
3. Recall an idiosyncratic gesture or behavior of the client's.
4. Identify what it was about this person's behavior in your office that you found so frustrating or that triggered feelings of impotence and exasperation.

(continued)

5. "Hear" the sound of this person's voice.

6. Really concentrate to recall a distinctive phrase or nuance that reminds you of this person.

With this client now freshly in your consciousness, clearly present in your heart and soul, quickly jot down the host of feelings and the variety of reactions going on within you.

- Hate (@ parents)
- Frustration
- Anger (@ system)
- Sadness
- pity

How Failure Helps

Although no therapist would willingly choose failure over success, there are, nevertheless, useful things that can be learned from such an experience. This is especially the case when the negative outcome or mistake is acknowledged and processed constructively.

Complete this exercise to help you explore the benefits of failure.

- Mention a time in which failure promoted positive reflection in your life.

    Example: "There was one client I was very much looking forward to working with, but she never returned after the second session. No explanation. After I recovered from my disappointment, I spent more time thinking about this case than about a dozen other ones in which things went well."

- Describe a time when failure stimulated constructive change in your life.

    Example: "I tried as hard as I could to get along with a few colleagues, but I couldn't seem to bridge whatever gap existed between us. As a result I started thinking on a broader scale; specifically, that maybe I'm not cut out to work in that

    (continued)

type of setting. That realization gave me the push to go out on my own."

- Recall a time when failure provided you with useful information about yourself or the world.

  Example: "I tried to sell an idea, but no one was buying. I must have been rejected fifteen times before I finally gave up. I learned that sometimes it's futile to keep setting myself up for this sort of disappointment when there are other areas in which success is far more likely."

  I have learned when I am extremely angry bk of a failure I cry. I can't help it.

- Note an instance when failure gave you valuable feedback on the impact of your actions.

  Example: "I used to confront people whenever I first became aware of some discrepancy or inconsistency. I thought I was being helpful, but lots of times my actions were misunderstood or ineffective. I learned to pay more attention to the other person's readiness levels to hear what I have to offer."

- Describe how failure improved your tolerance for frustration, or encouraged greater flexibility.

    Example: "I recently took up golf. I stink at it—can't hit the ball straight to save my life. But for the first time in my life I've decided that I can still have fun even when I'm not good at something. I've gotten to the point where I actually don't mind hitting balls into the lake or sand traps. The best part is that I've been able to generalize this learning to other areas of my life."

- Show how failure sparked greater creativity in you, and a willingness to experiment.

    Example: "I was teaching a class of the most unresponsive students I've ever seen. I couldn't get them to respond, or even to laugh, no matter what I tried. All of my favorite techniques failed

(continued)

miserably; I went through my whole repertoire. Still, no reaction to speak of. So I went on to invent another half dozen new classroom strategies I otherwise never would have even dreamed of. Although they still didn't work with this class, I was grateful for the innovations I developed, which I knew I could use elsewhere in the future."

Many of the therapists I've spoken to over the years report that they regard failures as gifts of a sort, in that they provide useful feedback to make adjustments. One therapist, in particular, believed quite strongly that you can't do good therapy if you aren't also doing bad therapy—meaning that learning from our mistakes is what teaches us to get better at what we do.

How many ways can you think of that failure can actually be quite helpful?

1. Brings you closer to God
2. Provides feedback
3. Enlighting (sp?)
4. Better serve the clients
5. understand own weaknesses
6.

7.

8.

9.

10.

Compare what you wrote to the following list of ways that other therapists report failures have been most useful to them. For each one, think of an example from your own life or work that might illustrate this concept in action.

- Failure stimulates change in that it forces you to try something different from what you've used before.

  Leaving Deaf Ed → counseling

- Failure simply represents useful information and feedback that allows you to make adjustments that might be more effective.

  APA citation

- Failure encourages greater creativity and inventiveness. You are required to develop a method or an approach customized to the situation, perhaps something you've never tried before.

  London Smith

(continued)

- Failure teaches greater humility, to accept your limitations while also strengthening resolve.

Justyn Bayer

Processing Failures

Failure can result in learning and growth when it is processed in ways that lead to reflection, flexibility, and changes in how you operate.

Think of a client you are seeing right now (or with whom you worked recently) that you would qualify as a failure. Keeping this case in mind, answer the following questions:

- What are the signs that therapy isn't working? How can you know for sure that what you're doing isn't helpful on some level?

The client isnt responding to treatment; not making progress / growth

Remains in a fixed mindset

Relapsing into prev. behavior / thoughts

- Some clients actually enjoy stifling progress because of the secondary gains they accrue, such as distracting you from real issues, feeling powerful thwarting an authority figure, gaining

The Therapist's Workbook

a sense of control over the pace, destroying things on their own terms, and remaining in familiar territory. What payoffs from failure might your client be enjoying?

- Remaining the center of attention
- Medication privelages
- Not having to face reality
- Control over others
- Power game / Chess game
  - Enjoy manipulation

- When did things start slipping downward? Re-create the sequence of events.

When the client gained control & I lost all sense of control.

- So far, which interventions have been most helpful, and which have been least helpful?

(continued)

- Who has an interest in sabotaging the treatment?

  Sometimes Parents

- How have you been negligent? Review your choice of interventions, as well as how they were executed.

- What issues or factors might you have overlooked?

  My participation in the power struggle

- What in you is getting in the way of your being more effective? How have your compassion and empathy toward this person been compromised?

  yes

- What can you learn from this experience to help you grow?

Do not get involved in a power struggle

Coming to Terms with Disappointments and Failures

More than ever before—due to funds being cut, certain treatment regimens being prescribed, and the severity of problems increasing—the therapist's job is becoming even more challenging. It is inevitable that you will face your own limitations. And all too often you will have to let go of a client you couldn't help.

Returning to the case you conjured in the previous section, in retrospect, what could you have done differently with this case?

Not engage in the power struggle.

What do you wish you could do to banish such "ghosts" from your personal space in the future?

PTSD = provide services to people & help them heal

Future Resolutions

Failures do get your attention in ways that nothing else can. They force you to examine the value of what you do. They compel you to reflect on your behavior and its impact. They are humbling experiences that remind you of your own limitations.

Declare here what you intend to do differently in the future when confronted with failure. ⌐

No touch
No eye contact ⌐   during
No talk   agression

Don't engage in the tit-tac

No power struggles!

CHAPTER 5

Clients as Teachers: Reciprocal Effects and Influences

Traditionally, the very idea of clients affecting their therapists was considered evidence of a lapse in judgment. We were supposed to remain neutral, enforcing clear and consistent boundaries, and avoid—or at least work through—countertransference reactions as they emerged. Any strong feelings we had toward clients, whether in the form of affection or distaste, were proof that we had lost our composure.

I remember working on a research project a few years ago in which we were interviewing some of the most prominent therapists and theorists about what they had learned from their clients over the years. Specifically, we asked the participants to describe the client who had impacted them the most, whether personally or professionally.

Bring to mind an image of the client who has had the most profound influence on you, either in terms of your professional development or in some far more personal way. Describe what it was about this individual or relationship that was so powerfully meaningful.

(continued)

WTF?!

Among the few dozen therapists we interviewed—among them many household names—was one hero of mine whose textbooks I had read as a student and later used as a professor. I'm not sure exactly why he agreed to participate in our study, because once the conversation began he readily admitted that in his five decades of practice he really couldn't think of a single client who had ever impacted him in any significant way. In fact, he told us that any therapists who do allow themselves to be so affected are clearly unprofessional, if not unethical. After the stunned silence that followed that declaration, he asked us whether we wanted to hear, instead, about books he had read that had had a profound influence on his development. We politely declined.

This therapist, now an ex-hero, is representative of the long-standing belief that therapists can somehow remain completely aloof and unaffected by their relationships with clients. The literature is filled with technical terms for these so-called lapses of control, whether called blurred boundaries, co-dependence, projection, overidentification, compassion fatigue, vicarious trauma, or secondary trauma. There is also the bias that any impact clients do have on us must be essentially negative, coupled with a very important prohibition that we ought not be doing anything to meet our own needs in session.

None of that means, however, that we don't profit personally from our sessions, that we don't learn a great deal about life, about the world, about ourselves, during the process.

What was it about certain clients that had a major impact on you in terms of your professional development or personal life? What was it about your interactions, or relationships, with them that was most important to you?

Novelty

Think about the people you have helped over the years—the dozens, hundreds, perhaps thousands of individuals. No doubt some of them are more memorable to you than others. Why? Certainly, novelty is one factor: The clients who struck you as highly unusual or interesting are probably those you remember the most vividly.

For one project, a colleague and I asked prominent therapists to recall the single client who was most memorable to them. Often, those they mentioned had presented with an issue or a behavior that they had never encountered before. My personal story involved the first client I saw while an intern at a psychiatric unit. The man wanted me to cut off his nose because of a disturbing smell he said wouldn't go away. Without providing too much detail, I learned this patient had been having a rather amorous relationship with a member of the bovine family (to be blunt, he was having sex with a cow) and feeling

WTF!

ha!

guilty about it. As a city boy from Detroit, I never could have dreamed such a thing was possible, not in my wildest imagination. Without thinking, I asked him how one consummates such an encounter (it involves a stepladder).

Not surprisingly, this is an example of a case I will never forget, simply because it was so totally new for me. I actually was able to help this man, and after just a few sessions, by avoiding overt judgment when I responded to him (but you can imagine what was going on in my head).

Novelty is just one variable that is associated with your most memorable clients. There are other factors as well.

Describe the most memorable or unusual case you have yet encountered, one that is likely to stick with you for years.

Why do you suppose this case is so memorable for you, out of all the people you have seen?

Being Witness to Profound Change

There is something about being with someone in the throes of transformation that is powerful indeed. Yet we are more than mere witnesses to the changes that take place in our clients: We are their companions on this journey.

I spend much of my professional life these days taking colleagues and students to remote parts of the world to work on social justice and service projects. There is no way that someone could experience such a trip and come back the same as when he or she left. On them, we face untold hardships and often suffer emotional overload. One of the reasons I do this kind of work is because I so enjoy watching (and leading) the profound changes that take place among my team members.

> Describe an instance when you helped someone and were significantly moved as a result of the changes this person underwent. In some ways, the experience changed *you* as well.
>
> Daniel Schwartz
> — taught me the labels we come in w/ are not the labels we have to leave with

(continued)

Experiencing Transcendent Empathy

By experiencing transcendent empathy, I'm talking about the kind of connection you felt with a client that went beyond an ordinary meeting of the minds. You achieved a level of intimacy that was profound, almost spiritual in its form. The limits you may formerly have thought restricted your connections with clients were shattered. You felt a closeness to your client, one that was neither self-indulgent nor excessive; rather, it was as if each of you could continuously understand one another.

Recently, I met with a young woman who was grief stricken over the death of a loved one. It was one of those sessions in which I lost myself completely in the encounter. Time stopped. I had what was almost an out-of-body experience, because it was as if I, as a separate person, was no longer in the room. I could hear, sense, feel what the woman was experiencing and was able to convey this back to her in a way that enabled her to truly feel my caring and deep concern. At one point she started crying, and tears welled up in my eyes, too. Although it now seems strange to be describing it in this way, at the time it felt perfectly natural. I will never forget her because I was so deeply moved by her pain; I could actually feel it in a way that was neither disturbing nor even uncomfortable.

Describe a relationship with someone you helped in which you felt deep empathy that went beyond anything you had experienced before.

Drama and Emotional Arousal

It doesn't matter whether the client expressed strong feelings of love, hate, anger, or despair, or whether you had powerful reactions of attraction, repulsion, frustration, or fear; such feelings tend to stick with you over time.

One of my most memorable clients was someone who had a dramatic impact on my development as a therapist. This was a teenage girl who was so depressed she would do nothing but cry throughout every session; she rarely even spoke. It wasn't only that her emotions were so raw and ever present; it was that I found myself resonating with her despair. I felt helpless and despondent over my inability to help her. And although it's been over 25 years since I've seen her, I still think about her and wonder how she's doing.

Describe someone you helped (or tried to help) who displayed or evoked strong emotions in a way that was unforgettable.

Captivating Client's Narratives

As mentioned previously, we are privy to some absolutely amazing stories we hear—dramas, reality shows, or situation comedies. The secrets that clients confess to us are often mind-boggling, and the challenges they've faced are beyond what we could ever imagine.

> Recall one such unforgettable story that haunts you to this day.
>
> *Casey Groom father attempting to kill her @ a young age*

Triggered Into a Personal Crisis

One final way clients can become our teachers occurs when something happens in a session or within a client relationship that sparks personal soul-searching. Unresolved issues from the past crop up in unexpected ways. Something a client says or does touches us in a way that brings up "stuff" from the past. Aspects of our lives that we have tried to deny or ignore make themselves known, and we must now acknowledge them. Parallel processes occur in sessions in which clients are dealing with issues that resonate within our own lives. When such a session ends, we are left reeling—not just from what the client shared but also from what is now percolating with us.

aka ripple effect

The lessons we learn from clients are often not those we would choose to learn—at least with respect to the timing—but we have little choice but to deal with them, in any way we can. One such episode occurred for me when a client was complaining about how boring and predictable his life had become. He desperately wanted a life more exciting and challenging but was fearful of cutting loose form his comfortable job and usual routines. Oops. I felt this crushing anxiety because what he was talking about was so familiar to me, to what was going on in my life. I couldn't wait for the session to end so I could somehow push this stuff back into its box. Alas, this was no longer possible. Not much changed for my client; he decided he'd rather learn to make small adjustments to his lifestyle than initiate any big changes. But for me? This conversation led to a lot of reflective thought, followed by major changes I made in my life. I quit my job. I moved my family to another region. In short, I started over again. I'm probably simplifying the situation by saying it was only this single session that sparked the changes I made, but it was certainly a major impetus.

Describe a time in which a sort of parallel process, or "ripple effect," occurred for you in session. How did a particular client challenge or motivate you to make significant changes in your own life?

Looking Back

Much of our development as therapists results not only from our formal education and training but also through supervision and personal therapy that occur throughout our careers. In addition, we read voraciously, attend workshops, and do in-service training to bolster our skills and add to our knowledge. We peruse journals for the latest research innovations or clinical applications. We talk to colleagues continuously and participate in case conferences to improve our professional effectiveness. All that said, the premise of this chapter is that it is our clients who often become our most important teachers. They are the ones who let us know, in the most direct and honest ways, what they like and don't like about what we do. If we are paying attention and take the time to continually assess the impact of our interventions with them, we are flooded with feedback from those we help. By their actions, as much as by their words, our clients tell us what is working best and what is not. In addition, because of the nature of the work we do, talking honestly about such challenging, deeply felt, personal, stimulating, sometimes forbidden aspects of being human, clients teach us a lot about ourselves. Their suffering—and their courage—often motivate us to look more deeply at ourselves and the choices we make.

Looking back on the exercises in this chapter, and reviewing all the people you have ever helped, make a list here of some of the most important and meaningful lessons your clients have taught you.

CHAPTER 6

Making Sense of What You Do as a Therapist

What therapists do for a living is help to make sense of the world, or at least the particular meaning of a client's experience. We help people to feel understood; far more than that, we assist them to apply what they learn in sessions to the most critical areas of their lives. In order to do this well, and consistently, we are required to have definite and informed notions about what works best. We are expected to have a degree of mastery over professional diagnostic systems, therapeutic skills, and interventions, not to mention the knowledge and the research base that form the foundation for what we understand about human development, learning, growth, dysfunction, and fulfillment. Then we are expected to adapt this learning to the unique cultural and individual differences of each client, depending on the presenting problem, context, and goals.

In spite of our great desire to understand what we do, not only for our clients' sake but also our own peace of mind, we live with considerable angst and uncertainty. If a four-year-old were to ask you what it is you do for a living (as my son did when he was that age), how would you explain that in the simplest possible terms? If you were asked to explain to a healer from another culture what it is you do, and how you do it, what would you say?

I found myself in exactly that situation while doing research in Namibia, with shamans among the Bushmen of the Kalahari. They are the originators of some of the most ancient healing rituals on the planet. For tens of thousands of years they have been practicing a form of "therapy" for a variety of problems. This therapy includes features that are typical to indigenous peoples across the globe, among them the use of movement, dance, prayer, music, chanting, spirituality, community gathering, and other rituals.

While interviewing the eldest shaman of the village, he asked me, through our translator, whether I, too, was a shaman among my people. When I answered in the affirmative, he asked me what it is I do exactly to help my clients. I told him that people come in to see me and they tell me their problems.

"Wait a minute," he said, a bit puzzled by the very idea that a man or woman would "come inside," since these people conduct all their practices outside, around a fire, with the whole community present.

I explained that sometimes the person comes with his or her family.

"But no community?" he pressed.

"No."

"And you meet around a fire and dance?"

"Ah, no, not exactly."

"What about the music and drumming?"

I admitted that I didn't sing, drum, and chant with my clients, nor did I pray with them and evoke the spirits of the ancestors. Anticipating his next questions, I also said that I didn't rub sweat into my clients' overheated bodies, nor press my fingers into their bellies to instill the spirit. The shaman became increasingly bewildered, so I decided not to mention that we also didn't press our bodies together, didn't ingest hallucinogenic substances, nor shake ourselves into exhaustion.

The shaman cocked his head and then, literally, fell down on the ground, laughing hysterically. Others from the village came to see what was going on, and when he shared with them what he had just heard from me, they all started laughing and pointing at me as if this was the funniest thing they'd ever heard.

When the old shaman had gathered his composure, he asked me what it was that I actually did with the people who came to me. I explained that we sat together while they told me what was bothering them most. We then figured out together what was going on and what they should do next to solve their problems.

"So you just talk to them?" he asked.

I nodded, uncertainly.

"But there is no music or dance or prayer? No community present? No fires lit to keep away the evil spirits and leopards?"

To each question, all I could do was shake my head.

"Tell me," he said, stifling another laugh, "have you ever actually *helped* anyone just talking to them?"

Good question, huh?

It did sound absurd, describing to my young son or to a shaman from another culture how psychotherapy works. And it does sound a bit strange that we don't really seem to *do* anything in our work except listen and talk to people. Yet it is truly miraculous how often this enterprise, within the context of a special kind of relationship, can produce stunning results. But how well do we really understand therapy, how and why it works?

How would you describe what therapy is, and how it works, to a shaman from another culture or to a four-year-old?

I listen to people's stories & try & make them feel better inside.

As we face the many challenges related to the clients we see, the colleagues we work with, or the setting in which we work, sometimes the whole enterprise of psychological helping appears absurd. But the nature of therapy is often ambiguous, abstract, complex, and uncertain, so feeling lost is not unusual; rather, it is quite normal. We attempt to help people who often can't articulate clearly what their problems are, using methods about which there is much debate and disagreement, and applying a process that we can't be sure is producing desirable outcomes. After all, clients outright lie or shade the truth about what they are doing, or not doing, in their worlds. We can't be certain that the changes we think we are seeing in sessions are real. And even when significant progress is made, we can't be sure it will have lasting effect.

It's no wonder, then, that we struggle with our craft. We may act as if we know what we're doing most of the time, but the truth of the matter is that sometimes we are faking it. Often, we don't really know how and why a particular client changed or a specific intervention worked. More than a few times each week we have serious doubts about whether what we are doing is actually making much of a difference. Worst of all, it is really difficult to get a handle on what we do that is most influential and useful. So we live with the reality of practicing a profession we don't fully understand. No wonder this presents us with profound conflict.

> Okay, time to be really, really honest. True confession time. Nobody will read this unless you decide to show it to them. What one thing do you tell your clients that actually mystifies you?
>
> "Everything will be okay"

The Mysteries of Therapy

Being able to endure, if not flourish, as a therapist is directly related to the ability to tolerate the inherent ambiguity of our work. Nevertheless, it's crucial that we understand what we do as therapists, so we can do it again, consistently and reliably, to produce desired results.

One way to continue on the journey to understand your own power and influence as a change agent is to start with the aspects of it that you are willing to admit are mysterious to you. I say "willing to admit" because some of the time we pretend to understand a lot more about what is going on than we really do.

When, for example, a client makes a dramatic change and asks me to account for what happened, I am delighted to jump in and offer a fairly coherent explanation, one that usually includes variables related to the client's motivation and expectations, the modeling I did, the particular kind of relationship we negotiated, and several specific interventions that helped the client to take necessary risks. Ask me later, though, how certain I am that what I related to this client is what really made the difference, and I'll hesitate a little, and probably have to admit, reluctantly, that I'm only fairly sure.

Challenge me once more, this time with greater intensity—"Yeah? And how would you rate your level of confidence that this is, in fact, what really occurred?"—and probably now I'll equivocate, saying something to the effect, "Well, this is what I *believe* happened. I mean, based on previous experiences, on a lot of research I've studied, and on some I've done myself, I'm reasonably certain that. . . . Well, I'm mostly sure. . . . Okay, I imagine that this is what *might* have taken place."

Although this later "confession" is more honest and accurate than my first overconfident remark, it certainly doesn't lead to a great deal of inner security about what I do that matters most as a therapist. The truth is, there is still a lot about this work that I don't fully understand. I can't make sense, for instance, how it's possible for two siblings in the same family, who both suffered repeated physical and sexual abuse, to turn out so differently and to respond to identical interventions in opposite ways. Likewise, I don't understand how so many therapists can appear to take such different approaches to their work and yet still get positive results. Nor can I get a handle on what it is about eliciting crying in sessions that often leads to such powerful, transformative changes. And I can't figure out whether I should stick to the present, delve into the past, or concentrate on the future. In sum, I don't honestly know whether most of the action in therapy takes place at a level of emotional activation or cognitive restructuring. Finally, I don't really understand why faddish new treatments seem to work so well when they often contradict what I've been doing effectively so far.

Along these same lines of inquiry, what are some aspects of doing therapy that you don't understand? List three that mystify you.

1.

2.

3.

Major Shifts in the Field

Even if you think you have a handle on what therapy is all about, how it works, and the most optimal way to do it in a variety of contexts, so many changes have taken place in the profession in recent years that it's mind-boggling to even consider making the necessary adjustments to accommodate them.

For one, managed care organizations have completely revolutionized the ways private practitioners work. We are no longer even referred to as healers but as "providers," which makes it sound as if we are technicians rather than artists, expected to provide some sort of standardized procedures on a predictable timeline. Agency therapists, as well, are under increased pressure to help people within sometimes ridiculously brief time periods. Consumers, too, expect quicker cures for their symptoms, if not with therapy then with medication.

I list several of the most dramatic changes in the profession here. For each one, note some aspect of it that you find troublesome or challenging. (Note: As with the other exercises in this book, these examples are not intended to shape your responses but to stimulate a high degree of honesty.)

- *Therapy as a business.* Greater emphasis is placed on efficiency, brief treatment programs, managed care, and accountability.

    Example: "Managed care organizations follow policies of capitation; they want more services for a modest, fixed cost. This results in my feeling like I'm working on an assembly line, without concern for the quality of my work."

    What happens when the therapy Rx runs out? who makes these decisions?

- *Technology*. Innovations in computers, media, and mobile devices have revolutionized the ways therapists do research, communicate, complete paperwork and billing, and even conduct sessions.

    Example: "I spend as much time staring at my computer screen as I do talking with clients and colleagues face-to-face. Maybe I'm more efficient, I don't know; but I do know I miss the more protracted contact I formerly had with people."

    I feel like people lose empathy skills the more they around technology & forget or how to effectively communicate w/ each other.

- *New paradigms*. Every few years we are told that our current theoretical orientation is flawed, if not obsolete.

    Example: "I just got back from a workshop on a new brief therapy. Pretty good stuff, too. But if this does what it's supposed to do, then what I've been doing all these years really didn't

(continued)

work after all. Maybe I should call all my clients back and tell them they didn't really get better."

who decides which models are ineffective?
Another tool for the toolbox

- *New research*. It's next to impossible to keep up with all the literature published each year; worse, much of it is confusing, contradictory, or incomprehensible.

  Example: "I've got a stack of journals piled up on my nightstand. Lately I've been avoiding them because the articles seem written more to help their authors get tenure than to advance the quality of my practice with individuals who so desperately need my help."

Who is really benifiting from
the ~~are~~ literatures.?

- *Cultural and gender sensitivity.* No longer can we expect to practice therapy without making dramatic alterations to account for the cultural context of our clients' experiences.

    Example: "I wonder sometimes if we aren't placing too much emphasis on how people are different, instead of on what they have in common."

    ↑
    this

- *Political correctness.* In the current cultural climate of our profession, there are certain subjects about which it no longer seems "safe" to have an open and public debate.

    Example: "The world is changing so quickly that I sometimes feel I'm being left behind. These days, I have to be so careful about what I say and how I say it, so I don't offend anyone, that it inhibits my effectiveness. And that's in case conferences! In my sessions, as well, I try so hard to control the way I talk that I've lost a lot of my spontaneity."

    you never know who you will offend by what you say

(continued)

- *Moral responsibility.* Increasingly, therapists are called upon to take moral stands, to fight against injustices—in some cases, even to censure clients and colleagues who engage in immoral behavior.

   Example: "I am torn between the need to be as nonjudgmental and noncritical as I can be and to refuse to tolerate attitudes and behavior that I consider unjust. If, say, a client uses offensive or racist language, I simply *have* to say something—I can't let it go. But then if I do, I worry I might be hurting whatever chance I have to help this person feel understood."

Active Ingredients

Making sense of therapy involves, to some extent, identifying which essential ingredients are most closely associated with constructive changes in sessions.

The variables that come to mind, which I think of as "active," should transcend specific theoretical allegiances or personal preferences.

This exercise is composed of five sequential parts, each of which builds on the preceding step.

First, make a list of all the ingredients and variables that you believe contribute to therapeutic growth and constructive change. You don't have to list the items in any particular sequence; just identify as they come to mind those that strike you as most often responsible for the dramatic, enduring growth that takes place.

1.

2.

3.

4.

5.

6.

7.

8.

(continued)

9.

10.

Second, revise your list by adding to it any of the following that you think are important:

Placebo effects: Setting up expectations that are conducive to positive change.

Altered states of consciousness: Fostering a mind-set that makes the client more suggestible and susceptible to influence.

Therapeutic relationship: Structuring a trusting alliance built on respect and caring.

Cathartic processes: Providing opportunities for the client to express feelings.

Consciousness raising: Encouraging the client to look at alternative realities and perspectives.

Cognitive or narrative shifts: Helping clients to look at other ways of framing and interpreting their experiences.

Power explorations: Examining and exploring the ways that gender, culture, socioeconomic status, or sexual orientation influence and shape beliefs and experiences.

Reinforcement: Supporting those behaviors that are fully functioning and self-enhancing.

Rehearsal: Providing opportunities for practicing new behaviors.

Task facilitation: Structuring learning experiences that make incremental steps toward desired goals.

Major demolition: Shaking things up so that the client is forced to develop new ways to solve problems or resolve issues.

Modeling: Demonstrating by your own behavior the values and behaviors that are most important for your clients to learn.

Third, take all the factors in your revised list and organize them into three or four different groups that make intuitive sense to you.

Group 1	Group 2
1.	1.
2.	2.
3.	3.
4.	4.

Group 3	Group 4
1.	1.
2.	2
3.	3.
4.	4.

Fourth, once you have organized the variables into groups, go back and give the categories names.

(continued)

Finally, describe how these principal factors are represented in your clinical work.

Discrepant Feedback

One other cause of confusion and frustration in your work no doubt derives from the different opinions you hear from various colleagues and supervisors about the best way to proceed with a given case. It is hard enough to live with the uncertainty that almost everything you do may be second-guessed; it is even more baffling to then consult a half-dozen experienced therapists and get just as many different answers to your questions.

Imagine, for example, the following brief interaction between a client and a therapist:

Client: Nobody can believe the way I've been treated by these people at Protective Services. It seems like they don't give a shit at all what happens to someone like me. I'm just another case file to them.

Therapist: Now you're having second thoughts about having contacted them in the first place. You're angry at them for not caring enough to do the job they should, but also at yourself for thinking you could trust them.

Now imagine that several experts in the field were watching this session behind a one-way mirror and that they commented as follows about the therapist's intervention.

The Therapist's Workbook

Supervisor 1:	A solid reflection of feeling and content.
Supervisor 2:	This confrontation seems premature.
Supervisor 3:	A bit obvious and superficial.
Supervisor 4:	This observation appears unwarranted.
Supervisor 5:	This brings the client closer to the real issue.
Supervisor 6:	This just enables rather abusive behavior.
Supervisor 7:	I'm unsure about what the therapist is trying to do here.

If so many different opinions can be expressed about a single interaction—whether it was essentially helpful, harmful, or useless—it means an even greater difference of opinion exists about many case conceptualizations.

Describe a recent similar experience of yours where you received contradictory feedback from several sources.

What do you find most effective in resolving such differences of opinion so that you can bring something useful to your troubling case?

Secrets of the Profession

Go to any professional workshop or conference or read most any book in the field and you will get the distinct impression that the presenter or the author has some fairly clear, definite, impassioned ideas about how therapy works. In addition, he or she believes strongly that the only legitimate way to do this work "properly" and effectively is to follow his or her lead. I've always envied, if not admired, such a deep sense of confidence, but it is far from my own experience of what it's like to help people.

I don't mean to say that we are clueless about what we're doing, and how and why it works. What I am saying is that there are many other possible explanations to account for the phenomena that take place in sessions, many of which we will never, ever truly understand.

There are secrets we live with, many of which we don't feel comfortable talking about openly. I'm not referring here to the secrets that clients share with us, but rather, those that are part of what we do. The public and our clients have certain expectations that we be self-assured about what we're offering. Such confidence even contributes to the placebo effect, whereby positive expectations lead to more robust change effects. Yet if we were being honest with ourselves, we'd have to acknowledge that much of the time we don't really understand what is going on with a client during the throes of our work. That doesn't mean that we aren't skilled at presenting reasons to explain what happened, and why, or that we don't have our favorite ideas to account for how change best occurs; it's just that we can also think of so many other theories that are equally valid.

We live with uncertainty every day. We sit with people who demand answers and push us to tell them what is going on. And we comply as best we can, offering interpretations and explanations that appear to be useful. But are they really, truly the definitive answers? That is only one of several disorienting questions we must confront as we attempt to make sense of what we do as therapists.

I reveal in the following sections some of the most common secrets that we therapists keep to ourselves.

Most of the Time You Don't Know What You Are Doing

How much of the time in sessions do you feel 100 percent confident that you know what is really going on and that what you are doing with a given client is exactly the right choice?

100   *The Therapist's Workbook*

I remember one client, a man suffering from panic disorder: He responded so well—in session—to almost everything I tried. My diagnosis seemed spot-on accurate. My interpretations hit their mark almost every time. Our conversations were lively and stimulating, and he was always grateful. The only problem, as I later learned, was that the symptoms hadn't actually abated. He was patient, though, and agreed with my assessment that improvement would come in time. Finally, we both agreed he had made enough progress, so we ended the sessions. A reasonably happy ending. (You should read my progress notes. They practically sparkle with assurance and definite answers about what we were doing and where we were headed.)

Imagine my dismay when, a few months later, the client returned to tell me that he'd just discovered he had a leak in his furnace and that once he got it repaired, his so-called panic reactions disappeared. So all along he hadn't really needed a therapist but a furnace repairman! I doubt this is the only time that I didn't really know what was going on but did my best to believe that was the case.

Allow the curtain to drop, just for a minute or two. If you were being really honest with yourself, what percentage of the time do you feel completely confident that you know exactly what you're doing with any given client?

How do you live with your uncertainty? How do you cope with the expectations that clients have about you—that you have a reasonably clear idea of what their problem is and how to fix it?

By worrying about it

(continued)

Even When You Think You Know What You're Doing, Others Disagree

How do we possibly explain the many different approaches to doing therapy, which all appear to work effectively? If that isn't confusing enough, add to the question how to make sense of the divergent approaches these approaches take. Some theories advocate working on cognitions, others on behavior, still others on underlying feelings. Some say that we should focus on the past, others on the present or future. There are theories that advocate talking, while others insist taking action is what's necessary. Others believe the best approach is to work with people individually, or with their families, or in groups. There are those who prefer interpretation, whereas others favor confrontation or support. There are literally dozens of empirically validated and carefully researched therapies that all appear to be doing different things.

So, even if you are one of the fortunate few who believe with all your heart, soul, and mind that you have discovered/invented/adopted the single best approach to therapy, hands down, I assure you I can find innumerable distinguished colleagues who could and would easily refute these most cherished beliefs.

Okay, yes, there are a few basic things about which all or most of us will agree. Everyone now acknowledges that the therapeutic relationship is key. Likewise, there is some consensus that relationships tend to work better when the client is treated as a collaborator, rather than as a passive subject; or that, usually, there needs to be more than just talk, that some form of active practice is in order. But aside from these basics, there is still active debate—seen in the literature and heard at staff meetings and professional conferences—over which is the best way to do this work.

List three ideas that you are most attached to, that serve as the foundation of your work. These are your most cherished assumptions about how therapy works and the most appropriate role for you to play in the process. You have accumulated convincing evidence from personal experience, research studies, successful cases, and intuition to convince you that these concepts are virtually certain to be significant factors in doing good therapeutic work.

1. Therapeutic alliance

2.

3.

Now play devil's advocate: Refute each of these assumptions/ideas by providing arguments from the "opposition"—effective professionals, deserving of respect, whose beliefs are diametrically opposed to yours.

1.

2.

3.

(continued)

How do you live with the conflict that no matter how positive you are that you are working in the best way possible, others strongly believe you are misguided, if not downright wrong?

You Can Never Be Sure If and When You Ever Help Anyone

This may be the most disturbing secret of all. It turns out that the clients we think we helped may not have changed at all outside our sessions together. Conversely, those we think of as failures might really have changed the most, but outside our view.

Can we really trust what clients tell us about their progress? There are some who report that they aren't improving, yet we hear from those who know them that they seem so different, even though the clients themselves won't acknowledge it. There are other clients who say they are feeling so much better, who thank us profusely for everything we are doing and tell us how much we are helping, yet they show no signs of change outside the therapeutic environment. There are also cases that seem like failures initially but that have delayed effects, sometimes many months later—and we never hear about them. And what about those clients who improve in all kinds of observable ways, but the effects don't last beyond a few weeks after terminating therapy?

Perhaps worst are the clients who flat-out lie. I've spent the past few years asking therapists to share their stories of clients who have lied to them in spectacular ways. I don't mean little lies of omission or slight exaggerations, since 90 percent of people admit to lying at least twice each day; I refer here to whoppers. I once saw a client for a whole year who reportedly was suffering from PTSD as a result of horrific combat experiences, only to discover that he may never have been in the army. And that's nothing compared to other stories I've heard—clients who claim they are dying of cancer but who just want sympathy; clients who *are* dying of cancer and never mention it; clients who pretend they are suicidal just to get under the therapist's skin. You've heard the diagnoses for such cases, if not seen them manifested yourself—Munchausen syndrome, sociopathy, Krosakov syndrome, borderline disorder. Less dramatic are the clients who lie simply because they are testing you, or don't yet trust you, or want to knock you off your pedestal.

With all that in mind, how can you really know whether you helped *anyone*? What evidence can you trust? Can you rely on client self-reports when they are often notoriously unreliable? How about your own perceptions of progress, given that you may have a vested interest in being unduly optimistic? What about behavioral indexes that purport to be measureable? That's all very fine, but they may not directly relate to the underlying core issues or even be significant variables.

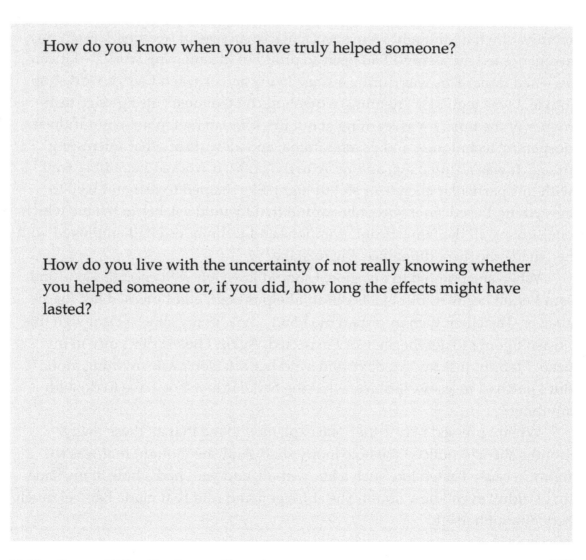

How do you know when you have truly helped someone?

How do you live with the uncertainty of not really knowing whether you helped someone or, if you did, how long the effects might have lasted?

Even When You Think You Helped Someone, You Can't Be Certain What Made the Difference

Whatever you do, don't ask. Yes, I know that we are supposed to be evaluating our effectiveness by constantly gathering data on what we do, and its impact. I am also well aware of evidence that indicates inviting clients to continuously provide us with feedback on our interventions is one of the best predictors of a positive outcome. I also realize, of course, that without such input from clients we would have no opportunity to adjust and customize our methods to fit the unique needs of individual cases.

With that said, there is nothing more disorienting than to ask a client as therapy is ending to share with us what we did that helped him or her most. Trust me: Most of the time you won't like the answer.

I recall one such episode with a client who was saying goodbye after months of what I thought were spectacularly successful sessions. Clearly, my arrogance led me astray. I had been so proud of the amazing work I—I mean *we*—had done. This was during a stage in my career when I was a workshop junkie. I was regularly attending workshops on the most cutting-edge techniques of the time. I was learning about Ericksonian metaphors, mindfulness-deepening techniques, and psychodrama, and all sorts of other interesting things. It was all amazing; and more to the point, it worked incredibly well with this particular client—or so I thought. She seemed to respond well to everything I tried. So it was only natural that I would ask her to tell me which one, among all the fantastic interventions and techniques I had employed with her, made the most difference. Big mistake.

When she pointed to my shoe, I should have left well enough alone and sent her on her way. But I just couldn't help myself, and I pressed her for an answer. The client then informed me I had a hole in my shoe, a clear sign that I wasn't going to get the answer I expected. Again I heard this voice in my head: "Jeffrey, just say goodbye and send her off. Don't ask anything more." But I just had to know. Besides, what the hell did my shoe have to do with anything?

When I pressed her further, she explained to me that all these many months she had noticed the hole in my shoe. And she thought that was so funny because I acted like such a know-it-all, and yet I had a hole in my shoe that I didn't even know about. She shrugged and said that made her feel much better about herself.

Of course, I thought, she's just denying and disowning the power of my therapeutic expertise. Right? I mean, she's probably dealing with unresolved anger issues toward me for her abandoning her. Right? My amazing interventions really helped her. Right? Not the damn hole in my shoe!

Well, I'll never know. And neither will you—and not just about my case but about so many of your own. The truth of the matter is that even when we do help people we can never really know what it was we said or did that was most constructive. If you doubt me, just ask a former client or student or supervisee years later what they remember most about your time together. Typically their answers will mention things we don't ever remember saying or doing.

Think of a time when you were certain you made a difference in someone's life. You were positive, beyond a shadow of a doubt, that as a result of your efforts this person's life was enriched in a way that likely could not have occurred without you.

What is your theory or explanation to account for the success of this helping effort?

(continued)

What are at least three alternative, equally valid explanations for what might have occurred?

1.

2.

3.

I think this is a fascinating exercise in flexibility and creative problem solving—to generate other possible reasons to account for phenomena that we think we already understand. I believe this is what keeps us nimble and on our therapeutic toes, flexible in our thinking, and much more likely to abandon ideas that aren't actually working in favor of others that might be more suitable.

And Speaking of Lying . . .

Sure it makes our jobs more difficult when clients deceive us or don't present honest and accurate narratives of what is really going on in their lives, but to some extent, we have to expect that. We have to acknowledge that, oftentimes, people don't know what the "real" truth is or whether it even matters. If a client believes something to be true, isn't that enough for our purposes?

Lest we become too critical of client deceit and dishonesty, we must also acknowledge our own lies. To the extent that the following statements apply to your experience, supply an example of each "little white lie"—meaning it is intended to help the client rather than yourself.

"I Know I Can Help You."

I don't know about you, but often, in early sessions with a new client, I really have no idea whether I can truly be helpful; yet I convey this optimistic message of hope.

> Describe an instance when you exaggerated your confidence in your ability to help someone in order to raise favorable expectations.

"Of Course I Like You."

I try very hard to like my clients when they are with me. But in fact, there are times I find their behavior annoying, frustrating, and even disturbing. Certain clients try very hard to make themselves as unlikeable as possible—or so it seems to me. Yet when I am asked, directly or indirectly, how I feel about them, I sometimes find myself offering false reassurance or evading the question altogether.

What about you? Describe a time when you expressed feelings to a client that were not quite honest or accurate.

"This Is What It Means."
We often give interpretations matter-of-factly, as if there is little doubt that what we're saying could be anything other than true. We often fail to qualify our remarks, or admit that what we offer is only a hypothesis or theory, hardly a statement of fact. Yet the power of our interventions is directly related to the confidence with which we employ them. Imagine saying to a client, "You know, I really have to idea whether this is the case or not, but maybe, or possibly, your problem might relate to something you said earlier."

Think of a recent example when you pretended to have much more confidence than you really felt when you implemented an intervention.

"Good Question. What Do *You* Think?"

Ah, the old deflection technique, to stall for time. A client asks us a question, a very good question, but we have no idea quite how to answer it. I remember a woman, a passionately avowed feminist, who wondered why her most frequent sexual fantasy was of being raped. Now maybe you have an immediate answer for that one, but I was totally stumped. Fortunately, our time was about up, so I could stall until I could consult with colleagues. (Not surprisingly, I got five different explanations from five different therapists.)

It's sometimes hard for us to admit we don't know something, not only because we want to appear smart, but because it is important for us to maintain some semblance of an illusion that we are wizards—it enhances our influence. Nevertheless, there are times we become very aware of gaps in our knowledge or competence, and we are afraid of admitting it.

> When recently did you find yourself in acute panic (or at least mild discomfort) because you were absolutely bewildered about what to do or how to respond to a situation, but were reluctant to admit it?

"My Clients Don't Lie."

I find this to be the most disturbing falsehood of all. I've interviewed therapists who claim their clients never lie to them; or, if they do, these professionals have total confidence that they can tell immediately. None of them would ever be using a workbook such as this—after all, they are already omniscient—but if they did review this statement, they would only shake their heads in wonderment at those mortals among us who can't read minds and predict the future.

Mutual Trust in Therapeutic Relationships

I'm not suggesting there's anything wrong with a kind of therapeutic evasion or deception that is intended to help clients—as opposed to meet personal needs. In fact, there are times when it would compromise our effectiveness, and the client's well-being, if we were completely honest.

The key point of the exercises in this chapter is to explore what it is that you do know and, conversely, what you really don't fully understand. Whether it is appropriate to share this with clients and/or colleagues is beside the point. Many therapists work in settings in which it just isn't safe to admit what they don't know or understand; they might be judged critically. And there are some clients with whom it is important to maintain at least an illusion of wisdom for the sake of their own belief systems, at least until such time that a more open and honest relationship can be fostered. The reality is that both participants in therapy (or any relationship) need to trust one another before more honest and frank admissions are possible. In the meantime, we do what we can to live with our uncertainty, with the complexity and ambiguity of our work, until such time that deeper understanding is possible.

For Review

Of the provocative and disturbing issues that I've presented in this chapter, which ideas, revelations, or insights about them do you want to hold onto?

Thinking and writing about these issues can be incredibly helpful, but *talking* about them with trusted colleagues or friends is an even more powerful tool. Identify someone you are comfortable enough with that you could spark a conversation with him or her about what is most interesting for you?

Finally, review what you know for sure: In spite of the differences of opinion that exist, and perhaps even fierce ideological battles going on, about the ideal way to practice therapy, there are still some things you know for certain about the work you do and the ways you do it. Summarize here a few principles that you are reasonably confident guide your practice.

PART II

Taking Care
of Yourself

CHAPTER 7

Addressing Countertransference and Other Personal Reactions

So far in your narrative you have been focusing primarily on the difficult challenges you face in your professional work and their impact on your personal life. You have completed an assessment of a number of these challenges you face and, it is hoped, clarified sources of needless stress. As you are well aware, insight can take your clients only so far; at some point, the time comes for taking decisive action. One way to begin this process is not to concentrate so much on your clients' behavior, or even on other external factors outside of your control, but rather to direct your initial efforts toward your own internal reactions to what you experience with clients, especially as those reactions interfere with your clarity and compassion.

It always is amazing to me that any two therapists can react so differently to the same case. An individual that one clinician finds to be a very resistant client might be regarded by another clinician as a delight to work with. The difference in response, of course, can be attributed to how each clinician views the client's behavior and, more importantly, to how particular buttons get pushed in the interactions.

Whether psychodynamic, constructivist, existential, cognitive-behavioral, or systemic in orientation, whether working with the past or the present, whether primarily insight or action oriented, most therapists recognize that personal reactions significantly affect the outcome of therapy. This is true with regard to how clients feel toward their therapists, and equally so with regard to therapists' reactions to their clients.

Signs of Countertransference

Countertransference is often defined as what takes place when a therapist acts out in some way in response to a client's behavior as a result of the therapist's own unresolved personal issues, biases, or exaggerated reactions. These inappropriate reactions can be either negative, as with clients whom the therapist dislikes, or positive, as with clients the therapist finds unusually attractive. Either way, the effects may be manifested in several ways.

Personal Examples

Each of the following signs and symptoms may be the result of a therapist having a very strong personal reaction to a client, one that is compromising the work. Supply a personal example for each one.

- You find it difficult to feel caring and respectful toward a client.

- You are bored much of the time when with a client and can't seem to concentrate on the sessions.

- You make a series of inaccurate interpretations of a client's feelings due to your own overidentification with the issues.

- You feel generally blocked, helpless, and frustrated when with a particular client.

- You have unusual memory lapses regarding the details of a case.

(continued)

- You have a tendency to speak or think about a client in derogatory terms.

- You are aware that you are working harder than the client.

- You find yourself more than a little attracted to a client, or to certain kinds of individuals who have particular characteristics (such as those who are wealthy or rebellious, those with curly long hair, and so on).

Who Provokes a Reaction?

Consistently throughout your career, no doubt there have been particular clients who have been able to get under your skin with relative ease. These may include those you find especially appealing. You may make allowances for them that you never would make for others. There are also clients who provoke in you rather strong feelings of anger, frustration, envy, pity, or impatience. Further evidence that these countertransference reactions are the result of your own unresolved issues is that not all clinicians react as you do to these same individuals.

In my own case, I admit, there are a host of clients who can walk through the door and immediately win my approval. I tend to warm up to those who dress casually (as I do), those who speak their minds, kids who are rebellious toward authority but within certain limits, men who cry fluently, women who appear poised and confident, clients who disagree with me firmly but respectfully, and those who struggle with issues I can relate to easily. Moreover, I tend to charge such clients less for sessions, demonstrate greater flexibility in my schedule, and tolerate more permeable boundaries.

Conversely, I am ashamed to admit, I have strong negative reactions to smokers, whiners, and clients who talk too much and don't listen. I have an especially hard time with those who appear arrogant or pompous, and who serve in positions of power and authority.

In the table here, make a list of clients who provoke consistently strong positive and/or negative reactions in you.

Clients I Like	Primary Reason for Reactions
Clients I Dislike	

Personal and Sexual Attraction

This is another one of those "forbidden" areas, where there is often a discrepancy between publicly expressed sentiments and privately thought and felt fantasies. There is absolutely no doubt that acting out sexual feelings toward clients is not a good thing. Simply, it is an abuse of power and a betrayal of trust. If not actually a form of rape, then certainly it is a form of emotional rape. Offenders can lose their licenses and even end up in prison.

In spite of the efforts we make to guard against acting on personal or sexual attraction toward clients, most of us are tempted on occasion. Almost every week, if not more often, there is some client who sits opposite you, giving you a starry-eyed, admiring, perhaps even seductive look. There is no doubt in your mind that this person would love to know you in a far more intimate way. To make matters even more complex, in a moment of candor, you might admit that you find this person immensely attractive as well.

Think about a client you are seeing right now who you find appealing in some personal way, whether physically, intellectually, spiritually, or emotionally. How are you aware that you treat this person a bit differently from others you see? This could be in the amount of time, attention, or flexibility you devote to the case.

How much time do you spend thinking about this client, perhaps even when you are being sexually intimate with someone else?

What steps do you take to manage your attraction to this client so that your feelings don't get in the way of treatment and you are able to restrain your own impulses?

Processing Countertransference Reactions

Before pilots begin takeoff procedures on the runway, they first go through a checklist to ensure that everything is in order. Flaps down (or up)? All engines functioning? And so on. In a similar manner, it is often useful when you encounter difficulty with a case to begin solving it by asking yourself a series of questions that assess both your professional dimensions and your personal reactions.

Bring to mind a case you explored in Chapter 3 of a difficult client who challenges your sense of competence. Once again, picture the person as clearly as you can, focusing in particular on the specific behaviors that trigger your most extreme reactions. Now, answer the following questions about the case:

- What specifically lets you know for sure that your relationship with this client is not working?

- How are you overreacting to what is taking place between the two of you?

- What might you be expecting from this person that he or she is unwilling or unable to do?

- How might you alter your working diagnosis in a way that seems more useful in this case?

- Who does this client remind you of, and how might you be distorting the way he or she appears to you?

(continued)

- Which buttons in you are being pushed by this client?

- In what ways are you making things more difficult than they need to be?

Avoid Blaming

Start with the assumption that conflicts are the result of two people contributing to the problem. Rather than blaming your difficult clients for being resistant or obstructive, assume that they are doing the best they can with what they have to work with at the time. In other words, they are trying to cooperate with you, but in ways that are different from what you expect or prefer. If this is the case, then you are an equal partner in the impasse that has emerged.

In any case that has become problematic, stop concentrating on the client's resistant behavior, the client's defenses and games; look instead at your own contributions to what has transpired. Furthermore, assume that whatever has happened in this difficult relationship is part of an ongoing pattern not just in the client's life but also in your own.

The self-supervision process in this exercise is intended to help you work through some countertransference issues that may be operating in difficult, challenging cases. In some questions you will be asked to focus on one client in particular who you find especially troublesome; in others you will be encouraged to look at ongoing patterns in your relationships with all your clients.

Identify Triggers

- What type of client has most consistently "gotten to you" in your career?

- In what ways is your competence challenged by these individuals?

(continued)

- How have you colluded with a client because of a countertransference attraction or overidentification with his or her issues?

- What do you expect of all your clients that they sometimes seem unwilling or unable to deliver?

Explore the Origins of Conflict
- What is the disagreement between you and your client *really* about?

The Therapist's Workbook

- How is this conflict familiar in your life experience? What does it remind you of?

- How are you experiencing a loss of control?

Commit Yourself to Act Differently
  - How would you like things to be?

(continued)

- How can you strengthen your resolve?

- What are you prepared to commit yourself to doing differently?

Experiment with Alternative Strategies
- What have you tried over and over again that hasn't worked?

The Therapist's Workbook

- Which of these strategies are you willing to discontinue?

- What are three things that you might do instead?

Getting Unstuck with the Help of a Partner

There are limits to what you can do on your own to work through difficult cases and countertransference reactions. Likewise, there are problems with some traditional supervision models in which you are expected to disclose threatening personal material to authority figures, who are also in a position to evaluate your performance. One alternative is a kind of peer supervision using the process described previously.

Peer Supervision Process

1. First, find a partner you can trust. Pick someone you respect not only for his or her expertise but also for the safety you feel in the relationship. List below the names of several candidates who qualify.

   -
   -

(continued)

-
-
-

2. Schedule some private time with this partner when you can describe to him or her your most difficult case right now. Because this process works equally well with any conflicted relationship, you may elect to work on a problem you are having with a peer or someone else. Whichever relationship you select, caution your peer supervisor that you are looking not for advice but rather for a sounding board to help you move through a series of sequential stages. Note below several salient points about this conflicted relationship that you wish to mention as relevant contextual background.

3. Define as clearly as you can several specific things this client does that you find most frustrating.

4. Shift attention from the client's behavior to your own internal reactions. What powerful feelings are elicited in you?

5. Ask your partner to function as a scribe and help you generate an exhaustive list of the ways you've already tried to work things out that have not been effective. Make the list as complete as you can; include everything you can think of.

6. Here's the hard part: Make a commitment, in writing, not to do the things you listed in step 5 anymore. If you are reluctant to make such a commitment, note those items on your list that you feel you must try one more time, to verify they don't work. Cross those items off your list. Put your signature at the bottom of the page. Ask your partner to sign as a witness.

_____   _____
Signature   Witness

(continued)

A sample list might look something like the following:

- Using confrontations to point out discrepancies between what the client says he/she will do and what he/she actually does.
- Trying as hard as I can to convince the client that he/she really has changed, even though he/she repeatedly denies it.
- Working harder than the client in sessions to generate alternative courses of action he/she can take. When he/she runs dry, I "rescue" him/her.
- Filling empty spaces in sessions by being overly responsible for what I do.
- Being overly accommodating in the way I schedule sessions for the client's convenience.
- Setting limits that I can't seem to enforce consistently.
- Using immediacy and self-disclosure to build trust.
- Trying to persuade the client to bring his/her spouse into couples therapy.
- Doing whatever I can to win the client's approval and endorsement that what we're doing together is worthwhile.
- Taking phone calls between sessions to hear reports of the client's dismal progress.

7. Brainstorm with your partner a list of options you might try to replace what you've been doing and that has proven not to work. This means, of course, that you will have to give up what is familiar and comfortable, to push yourself to be as inventive, creative, and flexible as you can.

Start by listing strategies that are the exact opposite of what you have been doing. From there, generate as many ideas as you can both think of. The goal here isn't quality, but quantity, because helplessness and frustration often stem from a perceived lack of options. Your partner's role is to elicit as many alternative suggestions as possible from you, not to do the work himself or herself.

Looking Back

Many of the processes described in this chapter lend themselves to being worked through alone, but sometimes it is more useful to work with a partner. Experiment with both methods to determine which works best for you.

How would you summarize your most difficult unresolved counter-transference issues that you intend to work on in the future?

When Therapists Act Out

One consequence of being a therapist is that we are often forced to answer our own searching questions. Just as clients sit quietly and reflect on their situations, we do the same, trying to work things out in our own lives.

Regardless of how much control and restraint you attempt to exert during your sessions, there are still innumerable ways that your personal life affects your work. Here is the question: In what ways do you catch yourself acting out? I'm not referring to anything along the dramatic lines that some of our clients adopt, rather, the innumerable little ways in which you might rebel against or resist the confines you feel.

Following are descriptions by a number of therapists of how the acting-out process happens for them. For each description that seems familiar, complete the dialogue by adding your own reactions.

Example: "Paperwork, paperwork, paperwork. I just don't do it. I let it pile up. I avoid looking at it. I hate the stuff. I resent the hell out of these people who tell me how I have to do my job."

Example: "I often feel so bored in sessions. Sometimes, it seems like I don't even need to be in the room in the first place since the client just drones on and on. I drift off into my own world, all the while nodding my head and pretending to listen."

Example: "I probably schedule too many things in my day. Make that, I know I do. Often I can't even enjoy anything I'm doing because I'm always trying to catch up."

(continued)

Example: "I notice that, lately, I don't seem to care very much about the quality of my work. Nobody else around here seems to think it makes much difference what I do, so I've stopped caring myself."

Example: "I have become more and more impatient and irritable when I don't get my way. This often happens in staff meetings, when I can hear myself being judgmental toward others who think differently than I do. And I especially observe this in my sessions, when I can hear myself saying to clients in my head, "Come on! Quit whining and get on with your life!"

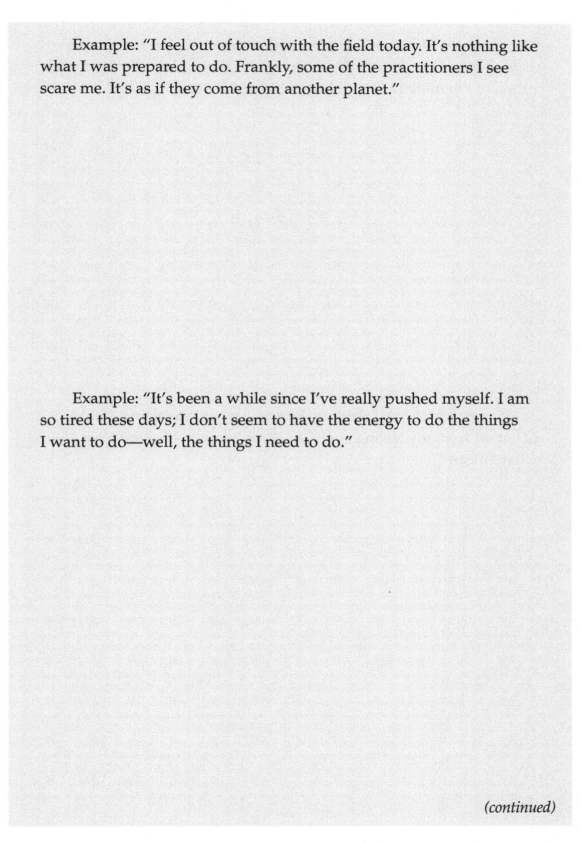

Example: "I feel out of touch with the field today. It's nothing like what I was prepared to do. Frankly, some of the practitioners I see scare me. It's as if they come from another planet."

Example: "It's been a while since I've really pushed myself. I am so tired these days; I don't seem to have the energy to do the things I want to do—well, the things I need to do."

(continued)

Example: "I'm pretty good at compartmentalizing the various aspects of my life. I don't think anyone at work realizes the kind of pressure I'm under. I keep things to myself."

Example: "Often, I don't really know what I'm feeling. I'm kind of cut off from my feelings, actually. I don't know: It's hard to say what I mean."

Further Work

Surely a few of the therapists' experiences from the previous section triggered familiar echoes in your own heart and mind. It is very difficult, if not impossible, to insulate yourself from the pressure and stress you are under and keep it from affecting the quality of your work.

As you think back on the various issues that were raised in this chapter, which ones in particular do you believe are most in need of some work in your own life?

CHAPTER 8

Avoiding and Countering Burnout

When therapists neglect themselves to the point where they not only lose joy in what they're doing but also lose themselves in the process, burnout may result. This is an insidious and progressive condition. In fact, the term *rustout* might be more appropriate, because a professional doesn't usually flame out all at once, in a single moment, but rather slowly loses interest in work and begins to exhibit the same or similar symptoms as those of his or her clients.

Typically, therapists who are already burned out realize that they are—they count the minutes of their sessions and the days until retirement—but many therapists may be showing early-warning signs of burnout without being aware of what is happening to them.

Assessing Burnout

Rate each of the following items on a scale of 1 to 3, with 1 indicating that the symptom is not present, 3 indicating that it is definitely present, and 2 meaning that you're not sure.

_____ I "disasterize" or exaggerate consequences.

_____ I find it difficult to stay present in sessions. My mind wanders.

_____ I am prone to fantasy. My attention is constantly diverted.

(continued)

_____ Increasingly, I am impatient toward my clients, colleagues, or both.

_____ I feel cynical, suspicious, and judgmental toward many clients.

_____ I sense a lack of support, or even active conflict or disagreement, with many colleagues.

_____ I am resistant to going to work in the morning.

_____ I am minimally invested in the quality of my work.

_____ I feel more than a little relieved when clients cancel appointments.

_____ Work seems like a routine—predictable, boring, and without challenge.

_____ I notice stress symptoms that are interfering with my sleep and other daily functioning.

_____ I feel isolated and alienated.

_____ I fantasize a lot about doing something else.

Add up your score, divide it by the number of years you've been practicing, multiply by your shoe size . . . just kidding! The total score doesn't mean much. What's important is that you've just reviewed the extent to which you feel burned out. The operative word in the previous sentence is _extent_, because burnout is not only gradual but falls on a continuum. Almost all of us feel burned out at times. It is a problem when it becomes chronic, leads to destructive behavior, and interferes with the quality of our lives and the effectiveness of our work.

In reviewing the various symptoms of burnout just listed, which ones are most problematic for you?

1.

2.

3.

Things You Can Do

Rustout becomes chronic, or flames into burnout, when you feel reluctant or powerless to make needed changes in your work or personal life.

Consider the following list of things you might do to prevent burnout or counteract its polluting influence.

- Initiate proactive changes in your work setting to create a more humane environment.
- Change the setting in which you do therapy.
- Reduce stress in your daily schedule by setting necessary limits.
- Confront the source of your negative attitudes.
- Begin studying a new kind of therapeutic method that interests you.
- Recruit a new supervisor who will challenge you in different ways.
- Make some new friends.
- Take some constructive risks; go outside your comfort zone.
- Spend a part of each day engaged in some type of meditative, reflective activity.
- Start or join a support group.
- Go to a retreat center to clear your mind and invigorate your spirit.
- Take an extended sabbatical and see another part of the world.
- Arrange an exchange of jobs for a period.
- Get into therapy.
- Redefine who you are as a person and/or as a therapist.
- Become involved in more interests outside of work.
- Reduce your debt and acquisitive desire.
- Go back to school.
- Get involved in a service or social justice project.
- Keep a journal about your efforts at recovery.
- Consider a new line of work.
- Complete a workbook for therapists that focuses on self-assessment, self-care, and self-improvement. Oh, you're already doing that one!

What are at least two actions you could take to counteract each of the symptoms of burnout that you checked off in the Assessing Burnout exercise? Don't limit the possibilities to only the suggestions I just listed; they are intended primarily to get you thinking about options.

1.

2.

Brainstorming Session

There is only so much you can do on your own. So get together with a group of trusted colleagues over lunch. But instead of talking about the usual topics, complaining about the same annoyances, griping to one another about the things and people you dislike, structure the conversation so that, together, you generate an exhaustive list of all the creative actions you could take to counteract burnout and prevent recurrences. Offer to act as the scribe, to write out the list; then duplicate it and distribute it to all who participated.

Of the new options generated in the brainstorming session, which were your favorite ones?

-

-

-

-

-

Other Steps You Can Take

In addition to the ideas that you came up with on your own and in your brainstorming session, there are several other steps that you can take to counteract burnout—or better yet, prevent it from taking hold.

- *Diversify your life:* What are some ways you can stretch yourself—for example, by developing interests, friendships, and leisure pursuits—so that all your satisfaction in life isn't connected to a single aspect of your existence?

- *Focus on the positive:* You make a difference in your work through cumulative effort over time. What, in your assessment, have you done that matters most?

- *Reach out to others:* Whom can you consult with as a resource? What are some ways that you could expand the quantity and quality of your primary relationships?

(continued)

- *Structure a healthy lifestyle:* What changes can you make in your daily regimen—in your eating, sleeping, and exercise habits—and how you manage your time that would improve your overall health?

- *Talk to yourself differently:* How can you reframe your predicament so that you don't feel as helpless or powerless?

- *Live how you advise others to live:* How can you take a stand for being more growth oriented?

Resolving to Act

Remind yourself to do one thing in the next week that will help you to resist burning out in the future. Make a resolution to reach out to a colleague who may be struggling with burnout.

CHAPTER 9

Travel That Can Change Your Life

True confession: I'd rather be a travel agent than a therapist. If someone came to me and said he wanted to make significant changes in his life, do it fast, and have the effects last over time, I'd have a hard time recommending psychotherapy as the first option. After all, it is mostly just talk for a few minutes each week, with long periods between sessions. During those periods, the client essentially remains in his or her usual environment, surrounded by the same temptations, and in constant contact with others who may not have his or her best interests in mind. Besides, it is, simply, really hard for a client to make permanent changes in life when many others may have a vested interest in keeping him or her the same.

I look back on my own life and consider the times when I have felt most troubled, as well as those when I have experienced the most dramatic transformations. In sum, I can say that as many times as I have been in therapy as a client and certainly enjoyed the process, the outcome of those experiences cannot compare to particular kinds of trips I have taken, from which I came back a profoundly different person. In fact, traveling has had a huge impact on my life, so much so that I've become an expert in structuring travel experiences for others in such a way that they are virtually guaranteed to leave the sojourner reeling.

I recall returning home after a month spent abroad, and while on the plane, trying to figure out how I could possibly explain to my family and friends that I was not the same person who had left. I had made new decisions about my life going forward that were based largely on what I had just lived. Let me add quickly that this wasn't a new phenomenon for me. Many times previously

I had felt myself irrevocably changed as a result of travel, beginning my first year of college, when I had been robbed while traveling cross-country on a road trip. I've also had near-death experiences: Once I almost succumbed to hypothermia in New Zealand; another time I fell off a mountain in Nepal. I've been terrified and lost in foreign lands. I've had encounters that have been so grueling and challenging that I had to reach deep inside myself to find new resources to get myself out of jams.

My own journeys have also led me to become fascinated by the ways others have changed their lives as a result of such travel experiences. I once conducted a series of interviews with people who said they had forever been changed by taking a trip that tested them in new ways. Often these adventures involved some sort of traumatic or challenging features that required the individuals to develop new resources or life skills that they were able to transfer to other aspects of their lives once they returned home.

Whether traveling to a foreign land or exploring new territory in your own town or city, describe a travel experience that permanently changed you.

It so happens that if you talk to people who believe they have been changed as a result of travel, you'll find certain elements in common in their narratives.

It turns out that the same elements in a life-changing travel experience parallel many that are inherent to effective therapy. No doubt you've noticed that people tend to embellish and romanticize their travel stories, making them sound more amusing, exciting, and even heroic. After interviewing several hundred individuals whose lives have been changed from such adventures, I've identified a number of crucial factors that stand out, many of which won't surprise you. In many cases, it is the experience of being, or feeling, lost that seems to be most memorable and enduring.

> If you were going to plan a journey for a client, one specifically designed to change him or her for the better, what elements would you include?

Based on the stories I've heard from people who report being transformed by a journey, here are the most common features among their experiences:

- *They did their homework.* They did some preparation ahead of time for the journey that included reflecting on their lives and future. Just as therapy begins not with the first session but with the first thoughts about seeking help, so, too, does travel begin with the anticipation and planning.
- *They were insulated from their usual influences.* One advantage that travel has over therapy (especially going solo) is that it takes people away from

those who tend to control and influence them most. This frees them up to discover new ways of being, or even to invent a new persona and try it out.

   • *They immersed themselves in a novel environment.* While it isn't necessary to leave the country or even one's town or city, the more novel or unique the environment, the more likely the traveler is to be stimulated in new ways. This is predicated, however, on deep immersion in that setting. As long as you stay at the Hilton, eat familiar foods, and move around by tourist bus, you may have a great time, but you will not necessarily experience much change.

   • *They moved through time and space.* The act of movement, exploring new territory, is what seems to get one's attention in ways that are difficult while sitting still (like in therapy). New sights, sounds, and smells all contribute to increased awareness—not only of the world but of oneself.

   • *They got lost.* As mentioned earlier, it is often the case that adversity, challenges, unpredictable episodes, even traumatic experiences teach people to be more flexible and willing to access new resources. The action seems to begin just at the point at which one finds oneself in an unprecedented situation, one that requires developing new resources and skills—hopefully the kind that are transferrable to other situations back home.

   • *They were emotionally aroused.* Memories are often more indelible when they are accompanied by strong emotion. In a way, the stress associated with journeys creates memory anchors that cannot be dislodged.

   • *They engaged in reflective solitude.* There must be time to reflect on transformative experiences, to make sense of them.

   • *They created meaning from the experience.* Here's where therapy comes in: People need the opportunity to talk about what happened and what meaning it has for them. Especially important is to figure out ways to incorporate new learning into daily life.

   • *They sought ongoing support and follow-up.* If the experiences are not processed and applied, they fade over time.

Change Through Travel

What I've discovered is that there are certain kinds of travel experiences that consistently produce the same type of dramatic changes that take place in therapy, only quicker. As a matter of fact, I'm convinced that particular kinds of trips have a lot in common with everything we try to do in our sessions.

Travel may be loosely defined to include any sort of journey that takes you away from your usual environment. It could be to a foreign land, but just as likely it could mean an adventure within a reasonable radius of your own home. The trips I have in mind, those that can change your life, have certain ingredients in common that will seem familiar to you.

For each of these life-changing trip "ingredients," cite an instance from your own experience that applies.

- *Mind-set ripe for change:* You changed because you were ready to change. You programmed yourself to change on the basis of your preparation and expectations.

- *Insulation from usual influences:* You were away from phones and computers. You were isolated from the people who normally influence you most. You had time to figure out what you believe, insulated from the opinions of others.

- *Getting lost:* The most transformative trips seem to be those on which unpredictable, unforeseen things happened. You

(continued)

abandoned the planned schedule and left the structured tour. You went your own way, even though you may have been lost part of the time.

- *Emotional arousal:* As in therapy, profound changes often arise when there is a lot going on inside you emotionally. It could be anger or fear or jealousy or joy. What is consistent is that the experience is intense.

- *Altered states and heightened senses:* You are most susceptible to change during those moments when you are hyperalert and open to being influenced. Ordinary events take on extraordinary meaning.

The Therapist's Workbook

- *Movement through time, space, and place:* Change often happens when there's literal movement, a prospect much more difficult to undertake in therapy where people sit still. It is novel experiences that capture your attention and force you to respond in new ways.

- *Teachable moments:* When you are traveling, you are open to experiences that you otherwise would not be. You are willing to look at the world, and yourself, in unique ways.

- *Facing fears:* Change often requires doing what's most difficult. Against your will, and without your permission, certain trips force you to face things you would otherwise avoid.

(continued)

- *Problem solving:* What we often attempt to do in therapy is make people uncomfortable enough so that they are compelled to adapt in new ways. Travel elicits these changes automatically, especially if you want to find food, safety, and a place to sleep. When things go wrong, you must make adjustments.

- *Creation of meaning:* The final stage of any trip, or therapeutic experience, that is significant and enduring is the time spent making sense of what happened. Just as important is how you decide to apply the lessons you learn.

Planning for the Future

The act of traveling, in and of itself, is hardly therapeutic. As much depends on how you do it as on where you go. As we bring this chapter to a close, give some thought to the kind of trip you might plan that could jumpstart your own change efforts. The particular sort of adventure you might plan will, of course, depend on exactly what you are looking for, or rather, on what you most need. Some therapists hunger for more stimulation in their lives, while others need a whole lot less than they currently have. Then again there are therapists not looking for much change at all in their lives; they might be quite content with the way things are going and would just like to make a few minor adjustments.

Regardless of where you are in your life and where you'd like to head next, design a trip you would be willing to commit to taking in the next year. Describe what the parameters of it might be, what goals you have in mind, and whether it would be best to go alone or with others.

CHAPTER 10

Building and Maintaining a Support System

Many of the problems we have explored related to stress, burnout, boredom, and inertia are traceable to the depth and breadth of support we have in our lives. Therapists are notorious for overscheduling themselves to the point where friendships and family relationships are put on hold or even neglected. Also, because we work with people all the time, especially individuals who are having very bad days, we are sometimes inclined to avoid contact with others when we might need them most.

Among all of the solutions that can be implemented to improve the quality of your life, none is more important than expanding your support system. This means populating your world with a rich assortment of folks who are both stimulating and loving. It also means nurturing those relationships in such a way that enables you to remain clear and balanced.

Inventory of Relationships

Let's begin by taking a look at some of your most fulfilling relationships.

- Who is your staunchest source of support at work?

(continued)

- Which relationship with a client stands out to you as being the most productive and satisfying?

This preliminary inventory should represent those of your current relationships that sustain you most effectively. They are hardly enough to provide all the support you need—and deserve—but they are models for what you care about the most.

Pushing People Away

Assume for the moment that one reason you don't have enough support in your life is because of things you do to keep people at a distance. Some of this behavior could be intentional on your part, although unconscious motives may also be operating.

Check the items in this exercise that apply to the way see yourself functioning in relationships, and supply an example of a recent time when you engaged in this behavior.

❏ Making yourself inaccessible to others.

Example: "If I don't go out much or put myself in situations where I might meet new people, it just isn't going to happen. Sometimes I can be a bit of a recluse."

The Therapist's Workbook

❑ Being critical and judgmental toward others.

Example: "I spend a lot of time acting cynical about the way other people behave. It makes me feel superior, but it also distances me; I don't give others a chance to know me, or me to know them."

❑ Seeking to control relationships in ways that make others become frustrated.

Example: "I like to think I'm pretty flexible, but in actuality I work behind the scenes to get my way. I might win the battle, but at great cost."

❑ Refusing to initiate contact or take risks with people I perceive as attractive or interesting.

Example: "When at social gatherings, I interact with the same familiar people, even though I'd very much like to make new contacts and connections."

(continued)

❑ Hiding behind your role as a therapist to prevent others from getting close to you.

Example: "I notice that much of the time I end up being the listener, the one with the answers. Yet even when people try to get to know me better, I deftly switch the focus back to them, because that's where I'm more comfortable."

❑ Being withholding.

Example: "I am withholding with my clients as well as with my family. I tend to pout when I don't get my way. I say to myself, 'Okay, you don't want what I'm offering? Fine.' Then I pull away to punish them."

❑ Refusing to invest sufficient time and energy in relationships; failing to make them a priority.

Example: "I say I want more support in my life, more intimate relationships, but I lack the initiative to follow through on my intentions. It's so much easier to remain in my comfortable, flawed little world."

An Action Plan

It's likely that as a result of reviewing how you might be keeping people at a distance and thus undermining potential for a more solid support system, you have discovered several self-defeating behaviors in yourself. To change this pattern, you are going to have to take decisive action.

What actions are you willing to commit to taking in your efforts to build a more loving and satisfying support system?

-
-
-
-
-

What are you willing to commit to doing to move what has been getting in your way?

-
-
-
-
-

Based on the commitments you've just made, identify sequential steps you intend to follow to achieve your ultimate goals.

1.
2.
3.
4.
5.

Watching Your Support Group in Action

For therapists, one of the familiar patterns that often emerges at work is to seek out and spend time with trusted colleagues. These are the people we eat lunch with, share a drink with after work, socialize with, or gravitate toward during periods of inactivity or times of need. Our interactions with these individuals are crucial to our well-being. They help us to feel less alone, better supported, and more securely grounded.

In some cases, however, the time we spend with confidants can make things worse as well as better. One of the patterns I've noticed when getting together with colleagues is that under the guise of being helpful to one another, we spend much of our time complaining about our lives—about how we are treated, about how unappreciated and underpaid we are, about the clients and colleagues not in our inner circle who make our lives so unnecessarily difficult.

Whether in the teachers' lounge in a school, the staff room of an agency, the coffee shop near work, or the bar down the street, therapists tend to spend a lot of time bitching and complaining to one another. Of course, this feels good; that's why we do it. The critical question I raise here is whether this sort of "support" is all that beneficial in the long run.

Identifying Consequences

What are some of the negative consequences you have observed as a result of getting together with colleagues to vent?

Among the negative side effects that therapists frequently mention as emanating from their discouraging collegial relationships are the following. Provide examples of those that may apply to your own situation.

- Reinforcing a victim mentality.

- Creating a climate of complaint.

- Investing energy in the negative rather than the positive.

- Engaging in circular interactions that lead back to where you started, rather than forward.

- Refusing to take responsibility for your own role, and actions taken, with regard to the problems under discussion.

- Feeling good for a short time, but then worse later.

Acting as a Process Consultant

What if you were to change how you interact with your collegial support system so that you continued to be there for one another but without the emphasis on whining and complaining? What alterations could you make in the patterns that mark how you currently spend time together?

Assume you are a paid leader or organizational consultant hired to observe your primary support group in action. What functional, as well as dysfunctional, dynamics and behaviors would you find most significant?

Most constructive and helpful patterns in action:

-
-
-
-
-

Most dysfunctional dynamics in action:

-
-
-
-
-

Making Recommendations

Once you have identified the patterns that seem consistently present in your primary support group, what actions would you recommend participants take to help them make their time together more beneficial, satisfying, and supportive?

1. Establish boundaries to make interactions more helpful:

   •

   •

   •

   •

   •

2. Set ground rules to make interactions more supportive:

   •

   •

   •

   •

   •

3. Alter patterns to encourage greater caring and respect:

   •

   •

   •

   •

   •

   •

4. Exclude certain kinds of content to keep the tone of get-togethers more positive:

   •

   •

   •

   •

   •

(continued)

5. Implement a new process to encourage a deeper level of sharing:

-
-
-
-
-

6. Agree on interventions that would keep topics of discussion focused and constructive:

-
-
-
-
-

Overcoming Obstacles

Continuing as the process observer and consultant who is studying your primary support group, what obstacles can you envision that might make initiating these changes a problem?

-
-
-
-
-

What actions would you recommend for overcoming these obstacles?

-
-
-
-

Time to Act

Collegial support is one reliable way to improve the quality of your work as a therapist, especially if the support group is organized around a few guidelines that create a culture of mutual respect and caring.

What do you intend to do to help change how the members of your current group of friends/colleagues interact with one another?

-
-
-
-
-

What steps do you intend to take to recruit from your community a group of interesting, compassionate, and compatible colleagues who can get together on a regular basis to provide mutual support?

1.
2.
3.
4.
5.

PART III

Practicing What You Preach

CHAPTER **11**

Accessing More Fun and Joy From Therapeutic Work

Once upon a time you began training as a therapist not only because you believed it would enable you to be helpful to others, to make a difference, and to eradicate pain and suffering, but also because you thought it would be really fun. Indeed, there are few professions that are more rewarding and that provide more opportunities to be creative, use one's intuition, take risks, and experience pure joy. Your passion and exuberance usually stem from two sources: the pride and satisfaction that come from inventing or executing a strategy that benefits someone in a significant way; and the sense of caring and pleasure you experience watching another person learning and growing, knowing you were an important part of that journey.

Too often therapists lose some of the passion they once had for their work. Their sessions become routine, if not stale. Their work becomes "just a job," rather than a calling; a business, rather than an honored profession. More and more often they find themselves less enamored by the challenges they face and more annoyed by the obstacles put in their way.

I firmly believe this fun and joy can be reclaimed. This is as true for experienced practitioners as for beginners. (Note, I am not talking about burnout here; rather, I am referring to when you are just going through the motions.) You know exactly what you'd say to a client who described a similar state. You'd give a rah-rah speech about how short life is and how precious is every single moment. You'd talk a lot about the value of taking risks, of exploring the unknown, of pushing oneself to explore new territory. You might even talk a bit about the limits we set for ourselves and how those boundaries can be transcended only by summoning courage and forcing oneself outside one's comfort zone. You'd press onward and urge your client to find more joy in work and life by making an ongoing commitment to pursue this challenging goal as a life mission.

Describe the last time you felt pure, unfettered joy as a result of helping someone—the kind of giddy excitement that left you barely able to hold yourself back from expressing your delight.

Taking Risks

We therapists tell clients that the only way they can make significant changes in their lives is by taking necessary risks, especially those that are unfamiliar and threatening. The same guidance applies to therapists who are feeling less joy and fun than is possible for them.

There are lots of reasons why you might avoid being more creative in your work and more inventive in your life. Check those excuses that hit home for you; then provide examples from your own experience.

❏ I "disasterize" or exaggerate consequences.

❑ I have a fear of failure, which inhibits me.

❑ I crave the approval of others, and don't want to disappoint anyone. I'm a perfectionist. If I can't do something the way I think it should be done, I'd rather not do it at all.

❑ I get anxious when I'm in a situation I can't control or for which I can't predict the outcome.

❑ I complain about the way things are and place blame elsewhere, rather than take charge of changing the situation.

(continued)

Next describe three activities in your work or life that you have been putting off doing because they seem risky—meaning that you have something to lose as well as gain.

1.

2.

3.

Now go back and select one of the three activities that you intend to do something about first. When you sense yourself balking or offering excuses, write down exactly what you would say to a client who offered the same reason(s) for reneging.

Favorite Techniques

Certain opportunities that arise in our work tend to be especially challenging and stimulating. For instance, I welcome those interactions with clients when they are resisting an interpretation or confrontation, and I can see clearly that they are engaging in the exact behavior about which we have been talking. I enjoy using immediacy as a way to get their attention and confront the behavior under discussion so that it can no longer be ignored. I especially enjoy creating metaphors that make maximum use of the specific details of the client's life—essentially, designing a tailor-made narrative fit just for that moment in therapy.

What are your favorite therapeutic techniques or interventions—those that energize you the most?

What would you describe as your "secret weapon"? This is your nearly foolproof strategy for dealing with client resistance.

Which sorts of clients or presenting issues engage you the most? These are the topics or situations that have you rubbing your hands together with delight in anticipation of addressing them.

(continued)

What would it take for you to incorporate into other areas of your work more of the pleasure and satisfaction you feel when using the aforementioned techniques in working with these clients?

Uses of the Self

Many therapists have discovered that one way they can inject more zest and excitement into their work is to stop trying to imitate the "masters" and instead continue to evolve their own style of practice, one that fits their personality and personal approach like a glove. For experienced therapists, this often requires incorporating their "selves" more into their work.

For you this means that rather than relying only on the technology of helping, you put more of your "self" into sessions. This doesn't refer to being self-indulgent or meeting your own needs. On the contrary, I'm talking about being even more sensitive to clients' needs, at every moment. It means trusting yourself and your clinical judgment more, and working hard to make necessary adjustments when your "felt sense" is not accurate. Most important, it means to stop trying to be like others, in order to become more yourself.

For each of the following strategies, describe one way that you could incorporate your "self" more into your work to experience more joy from what you are doing.

- *Intuitive assessment*: This refers to relying not only on your clinical training, your supervisor's judgments, and other sources consulted, but also on your own intuitive sense about what might be going on.

- *Transcendent empathy*: This refers to those magical moments in therapy when it seems that you and your client can read one another's minds and hearts.

- *Immediacy*: There are few interventions more powerful than when you share, in the moment, what you are experiencing with a client.

- *Self-disclosure*: Appropriate, timely, and brief revelations when you share something from your own life with a client can build trust, model effective behavior, and/or encourage identification.

(continued)

- *Structured demonstrations*: Sessions become more animated and lively when you put more energy into them. This means showing as well as telling. Don't just talk about issues; act out possible solutions or approaches to problems.

Creating Joy

As you look back on the thoughts you've had and writing you've done in this chapter, what do you resolve to do differently to generate more fun and joy in your work and life?

I resolve to:

-
-
-
-
-

The Therapist's Workbook

CHAPTER 12

Promoting Creative Breakthroughs

Now that you've finished the end of this chapter, what have you learned from it that dramatically changed your life and the way you think about your work? Of all the interesting stories told, the concepts introduced, the innovative ways offered to look at therapy and the way it could work once you released the traditional bonds of practice, what do you believe will stay with you, have lasting effect on your work and life?

List below all the amazing new insights you gained from completing this chapter. I'm serious! Do that now.

You might think this is a rather unusual way to begin a chapter, but I do it to illustrate the value of turning things upside down—to challenge the basic assumptions of what we do and why we operate according to established practices. I will sometimes *begin* a workshop by asking participants to imagine that it has just *ended* and to report on what they learned. This is just another way to get them to declare what they expect and hope to get out of the workshop.

Many of the conventional "rules" governing how we do therapy have little to do with maintaining ethical standards or protecting client safety; rather, they have become part of our tradition, which undergoes little critical scrutiny. Who says that sessions should be 50 minutes long, for example? Who says that therapy has to take place sitting still in chairs? Many of the most innovative therapists have sent their clients out into the world to accomplish tasks or face challenges. Most healers throughout much of the world believe that it is not through talk that change takes place, but through action, especially the kind that involves some form of movement, community engagement, and therapeutic journey.

Some of our field's most innovative figures, such as Virginia Satir, Jay Haley, Milton Erickson, Carl Whitaker, and Fritz Perls, were noted for their willingness to do almost *anything* to motivate clients to do things that were in their best interest. Rather than following the tradition of innovation among leading theorists, we try to emulate their principles exactly.

- Carl Rogers's notion of core empathy has been converted into a series of simple reflective skills.
- Milton Erickson's complex, intuitive interventions have been translated into training for developing metaphors.
- Fritz Perls's legacy has been reduced to a few techniques, like the empty chair.

I'm not suggesting that we all have the capacity or the interest to develop a new approach to therapy; I am saying that each of us has within us tremendous creative resources, which often remain unused and unexplored as we go about imitating others.

Some of us may be intimidated by the idea of being creative, which sounds as if it requires having an inborn gift. In fact, most creativity is derivative and incremental; it rarely comes as a major breakthrough.

Describe a small act of creative adaptation that you tried this week, whether it was successful or not.

I'm not suggesting that you become more creative in your sessions because you are tired of what you are currently doing or wish to amuse yourself. I'm recommending that you invent or adapt an unusual approach or strategy for the purpose of helping clients break free of their personal constraints. So often, just like our clients, we become stuck in routines, and find ourselves doing the same things the same way because they're familiar or comfortable. But the growth edge for our work, and our lives, is directly related to our willingness to experiment and be flexible. In one sense, we can think of a therapy session as a musical composition or a work of art: Each is unique; each represents a collaboration between participants to create an experience that may be unlike any other that has ever occurred. That is what makes what we do so exciting and endlessly interesting—unless we get stuck in our conventional routines.

What do you see as obstacles to your becoming significantly more creative in your work—and in your life? List them below.

There are several obstacles that often get in the way of our being more creative, most notably the fear of taking risks. We do what is comfortable and "proven" because it is safe, because we've tried it before and know that it works. It might actually have limited use or effectiveness, but at least we know we won't hurt anyone or "get in trouble."

When interviewing prominent therapists for a book about what leads most consistently to creative breakthroughs, several of them mentioned as the source of their innovation their willingness to take risks. To give just two examples:

1. Cloe Madanes, an innovator of family therapy, said she believes that most therapists lack courage, that they are so afraid of doing something wrong or getting in trouble that they play it safe, even when doing so is not in their clients' best interests.

2. Madanes's belief was echoed by psychiatrist and couples specialist, Frank Pittman, who told me that you can't do good therapy unless you are making lots of mistakes and taking lots of risks. He shared his experience of presenting a demonstration on stage with a family, in which

he took a very provocative approach. It proved to be widely misunderstood and dramatically rejected (the family walked off stage and the audience was appalled). When I asked him how he lived with himself after that humiliation, Pittman just shrugged: "You win a few and you lose a few."

Of course, prominent therapists can dare to be more creative and innovative, and to do things that beginners should never attempt. And there are some very good reasons why certain safeguards are in place to prevent professionals from operating outside the bounds of accepted standards of care. I am not advocating that we should all throw out best practices, those that have been supported by research and years of clinical experience; rather, I am suggesting that there are an infinite number of ways that we can continue to function at the highest ethical standards and still take our work to the next level. This is especially the case with so-called hopeless cases or chronic problems that have been resistant to previous interventions.

Your Most Creative Case

Describe the most creative strategy you've ever employed to help someone.

(continued)

What were the features of this relationship or situation that allowed you to be so creative?

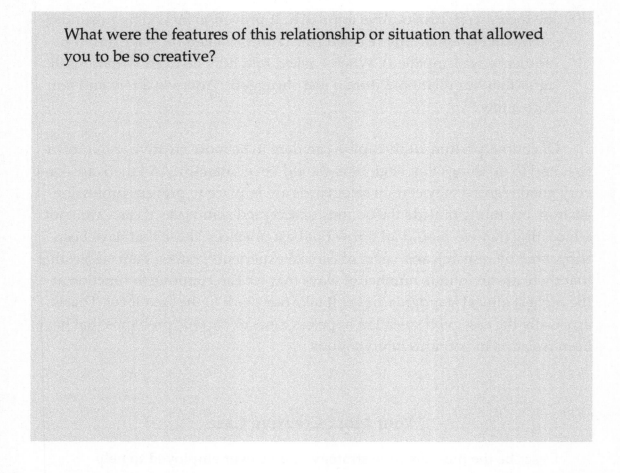

What It Takes to Become More Creative

What do you think would be required for you to become a *lot* more creative in your work and your life? Based on interviews conducted with some of the field's most wildly innovative theorists and practitioners, in the next exercise I list a number of the factors they indicated lead most often to creative breakthroughs. For each of them, see if you can supply an example from your own work or life.

This is an exercise in celebrating creativity, so if you can't think of an example, make one up! Pretend, for example, that you have a lot more experience initiating breakthroughs than you give yourself credit for.

- *Use a different kind of therapy for each client:* Creativity is most easily fostered when you adapt/change/transform what you already know into something original.

    Describe an instance in which you broke loose from your usual mode of operation and made some adjustment, adaptation, or improvisation that uniquely fit the needs of a client and particular situation.

- *Develop mutual trust:* In order for a therapist to take the necessary risks associated with creative breakthroughs, there must be mutual trust in the relationship.

    Describe a time when you felt particularly safe with a client, such that you were willing to experiment with approaches you'd never tried before.

- *Be collaborative:* Creativity is a collaborative process in therapy. It isn't just what the therapist does, but rather what both partners do together to invent something quite unusual.

(continued)

Describe a particularly effective collaboration you've had with a client.

- *Admit you're lost:* Unless you are willing to acknowledge that you have run out of available options, that you are operating in unknown territory, you aren't likely to find new ways out of the dilemma.

    Describe a time when being, or feeling, lost led to a new breakthrough for you or your client.

- *Embrace mystery:* It turns out that making sense of things and promoting deeper understanding isn't always the best approach to dealing with life's challenges. Among many indigenous healing traditions, the goal is to honor the mysteries we face, rather than trying to unravel them.

Describe an inscrutable incident when instead of trying to reduce complexity, chaos, or ambiguity, you honored it, leading to a creative result.

- *Question your most cherished assumptions:* So many of the world's great discoveries and inventions took place because someone decided to challenge the status quo.

    Describe a time when you questioned conventional wisdom and it led to a breakthrough.

- *Set flexible boundaries:* This is tricky because boundaries are established and enforced in therapy for very good reasons: to protect the client and the therapist, to set reasonable expectations, to provide a "holding environment," and so on. Yet many therapists report having unusually effective breakthroughs with supposedly lost causes only after they stepped outside their usual roles and challenged clients' expectations.

(continued)

Describe a time you broke one of your own "rules" and it ended up having a quite remarkable effect.

- *Develop cognitive flexibility:* One of the common tests of creative potential is "fluency," that is, the ability to generate multiple solutions to a problem, even some that might not make sense initially. After all, a number of the most interesting and exciting discoveries (e.g., X rays, Velcro, penicillin, Teflon, plastic, Post-It Notes, to name a few) occurred by accident.

  Describe a time you developed a really unusual, even crazy-seeming, idea in your work or life and it led to a breakthrough.

- *Demonstrate courage and constructive risk taking:* As mentioned earlier, being creative requires daring, at times even audacity, and a willingness to experiment with approaches that don't have predictable outcomes. Of course, such risks should not jeopardize client safety (and this is less likely to occur when a stable alliance has been established).

Describe a time you showed courage in your work and it led to a breakthrough.

- *Enter a "flow state"*: Creativity often takes place when you can get in a "zone," an extraordinary reality or altered state of consciousness that opens you up to possibilities you hadn't considered before.

  Describe a time when you entered a "zone," to remarkable effect.

- *Accept failure*: The reality is that most creative attempts don't work out as expected or hoped. Failure is inevitable and so must be accepted as part of the ongoing process of discovery.

  Describe a time you tried something creative that didn't work out well, though it did lead to some kind of advancement.

One of the most inspiring ideas that came for me as a result of talking to the field's most creative innovators confirmed what other research had uncovered: Creative breakthroughs are more likely to occur for those who show extraordinary commitment and dedication to their work. So-called geniuses in any field aren't lucky; they just work harder than everyone else.

For those who don't think of themselves of particularly creative or inventive, this is a message of hope. In many different professions, those who achieved eminence did so not just because they were blessed with innate ability but because of their sustained initiative. In the world of cycling, Lance Armstrong was among the first to scout each stage of the Tour de France before the day of the race, a strategy that others found too much trouble. Before the Beatles ever arrived in the United States, they practiced on stage for tens of thousands of hours, refining their act and musical skills. In our own field, the most accomplished therapists I know spend hours each week studying the sessions of other practitioners, trying to unearth the essence of their power. They are never satisfied with their level of skill or ability; they work constantly to improve, going far beyond collecting continuing education credits.

Thinking Outside the Box

All of us have had inspiring mentors, men and women we wished to emulate. In addition, we have inherited traditions that have been passed down from generations of previous therapists who have established over time the conventions we currently practice. Yet when you think about it, there's nothing inherently logical about it; there is nothing etched in stone that says psychotherapy must be structured in a particular way. As mentioned earlier, there is no compelling evidence that the ideal length of a session is 50 minutes, or any other consistently prescribed duration. And why is therapy usually defined as a conversational interaction, as opposed to another form of communication? Throughout the rest of the world, healing takes place within very different structures and in very different contexts.

Imagine that therapy has not yet been invented. You are empowered to develop a way to help people who are suffering from a variety of psychological/interpersonal problems. Forget everything you think you know and accept about existing treatments. Let your imagination run rampant. If you could start from scratch and invent your own system for helping people, without regard for traditions, norms, rules, and established conventions, what would your method/strategy/process look like? Think outside the box; let go of all you think, know, believe, and understand. Put aside your previous assumptions.

It was the philosopher Arthur Schopenhauer who observed that a creative genius is one who not only hits a target that others can't reach, but also one that most others can't even see.

ABOUT THE AUTHOR

Jeffrey Kottler has worked as an educator and a psychologist in numerous and diverse settings, including a preschool, middle school, mental health center, crisis center, university, community college, orphanage, corporation, private practice, and NGOs. A Fulbright scholar, Jeffrey has held the position of Senior Lecturer in Peru, Thailand, and Iceland and of Visiting Professor in New Zealand, Australia, Hong Kong, Singapore, and Nepal. He is currently Professor of Counseling at California State University–Fullerton, as well as co-founder of Empower Nepali Girls (www.EmpowerNepaliGirls.org), an organization that provides educational scholarships for lower-caste, at-risk girls in Nepal.

A prolific author, Jeffrey has written more than 80 books, which have been translated into more than 15 languages. Used in universities around the world, they are considered classics among practicing teachers, counselors, psychologists, health professionals, and social justice advocates. Some of his most highly regarded works, published by John Wiley & Sons, Inc., include: *On Being a Therapist, Creative Breakthroughs in Therapy, The Mummy at the Dining Room Table: Eminent Therapists Reveal Their Most Unusual Cases and What They Teach Us About Human Behavior, Compassionate Therapy, Beyond Blame, Divine Madness: Ten Stories of Creative Struggle,* and *Changing People's Lives While Transforming Your Own: Paths to Social Justice and Global Human Rights.*